Stranger on the Shore

Stranger on the Shore

JOHN SYMONS

SHEPHEARD-WALWYN (PUBLISHERS) LTD

2013 → Plymouth

First published in 2009 by
Shepheard-Walwyn (Publishers) Ltd
15 Alder Road
London SW14 8ER

British Library Cataloguing in Publication Data
A catalogue record of this book
is available from the British Library

ISBN: 978-0-85683-264-2

Typeset by Alacrity, Chesterfield, Sandford, Somerset
Printed and bound in the United Kingdom through
s|s|media limited, Wallington, Surrey

For Judy
who never met Dad

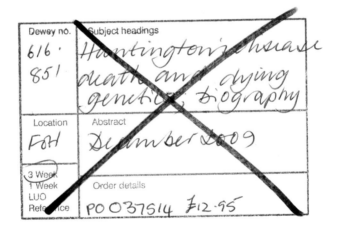

Contents

List of Plates

PART ONE

1
Dad

THE WOODEN scrubbing brush, with its sharp, spiky bristles, moves to and fro on the kitchen table. A little crescent wave of shallow water flows in front of it. And gripping the brush firmly and wielding it vigorously, in those days, were Dad's hands. There is a rubbing, grating sound, so intense is his effort.

You might catch a glimpse of a pale blue and red tattoo on Dad's inner arm, in the gap above the button of his shirtsleeve. Dad nearly always wore his sleeves rolled down. The table was of pine, before pine became fashionable; before fashion existed where we lived. Dad used to scrub it every week. He bent low over it – for he was a little over six feet tall – working with a block of hard green or yellow soap in his left hand, and all his elbow grease.

The table stood in the kitchen by the window, opposite the Rayburn that was Dad's pride and joy. Ralf and I used to play under it, imagining that it was a spaceship. We made a little control panel from a block of wood to which we nailed a few revolving wheels from one of the carriages of our clockwork train set. We sat there, partly hidden by the tablecloth, sometimes with our dog Patch, as we cruised around the Universe, or at least our solar system, in this makeshift cabin. We were good brothers, two and a half years between us, and I the elder, and we took it in turns to play the Captain, called Toby. All of this happened in the days before *Journey Into Space* created a sensation on the BBC Light Programme; but by then there had already been a space serial broadcast from Scotland, *The Lost Planet* by Angus MacVicar, on Children's Hour on the West of England Home Service. We listened intently to that serial as we ate our tea-time bread and jam, sitting at the kitchen table. For me, space travellers spoke in educated Scottish accents. It seemed inevitable, in due course, that Neil Armstrong, the first man on the Moon, should come from a Scottish family.

With a tie around his waist in place of a belt to make fast his corduroy trousers, fawn and well worn, and wearing a shirt without its collar, Dad came to grips with the stains made by our pencils or crayons, or the splashes from our plates.

It was Dad who inspired our game just as much as did *The Lost Planet*. One week in three Dad worked a nightshift, and he loved to observe the positions of the stars and planets as they changed through the seasons. He read a good deal about astronomy, and on the last day of each month he used to order *The Times* as well as his copy of *The Daily Telegraph* because it carried a long article about the night sky in the coming month. He used to talk to me about space and time, creation, and the wonders of life and the Universe.

Dad was always ashamed of the tattoos on his arms and chest. It was a 'silly thing', he thought, done by him in his earliest Army days. After he came back to England from India in 1947, after twenty-five years there, Dad never swam. Mum told us (and Ralf and I believed her) that that was because the sea was too cold for him here – and perhaps it was – but now I can understand that it was also because of that sad sense of shame.

It was sad partly because Dad's first words were remembered in his family as, 'I could SWUM!' He was only three years old at the time that he said this to his mother and father, who like their forebears for generations, probably centuries, worked a precarious living from the waters around West Cornwall. His mother had told him not to go into the water until he could swim, a typical piece of Cornish drollery. In his youth, his sister told me, Dad became such a powerful swimmer that he could swim to St Michael's Mount and back from Newlyn Harbour, about six miles, and in the Army he was a superb athlete. But in my childhood, on holiday at the seaside, Dad held our towels on the shore and waited at the water's edge while we swam.

In fact, I loved the pale colours and the fading shapes of the tattoos. Dad was happy to let them be seen briefly sometimes in the summer when, with his sleeves rolled up, he swept the garden paths.

As his hands wield the scrubbing brush, easing out all the grease and dirt of the past week, sometimes both hands together, sometimes just the right, you can see that they are browned by the sun of all his years in India: strong and hard hands, yet also gentle and sensitive. They have undertaken all manner of work of the heaviest sort in Cornwall, in Ireland and in the East. They have gripped a pewter beer tankard as he sat outside his tent in the heat of the jungle. But they have also carefully turned the pages of the *Book of Common Prayer* and the Bible at worship in St Peter's Church at Saugor, in the Central Provinces of India, and they have received the elements of the Holy Communion. They held his mother in an embrace during the last hours of her life and comforted her. They received his first son with delight from Mum when she presented me to him outside his bungalow in India in February 1946 (Plate 9). I can see the joy and humour in his face in the photographs of that event. He had waited forty-four years for children of his own. You can see the same character in his face that you sense in his hands.

A young boy does not set out to take in the nature of his father's hands, but for me the impression of that memory is strong.

There is only one photograph of Dad with his mother and his six sisters (Plate 4). All seven children are gathered around Florence Louisa, perhaps on the day of her husband William's funeral in November 1914. There is no photograph of all eight of the family together with William, who had been a fisherman and a member of the Royal Naval Volunteer Reserve. His death followed some early action at sea in the First World War. But there at the focal point, the golden section, of this single photograph of his family rests Dad's right hand – gently, firmly – on Florence Louisa's left shoulder, comforting and reassuring her. He was not yet thirteen years old.

And there it is again, resting lightly on my right shoulder in another photograph, taken in 1951 or 1952 when I was six years old. My cousin John, who, unknowingly, will play a decisive role in this story, took the snap. The four of us – Dad, Mum, Ralf and I – are standing in front of a line of trees. We had been gathering mushrooms. Dad's left hand, cupped to hold some of them, is on my left shoulder, and his trilby hat is partly visible, lying on the lush grass to our right. Beyond the trees, in the valley of the River Plym, our village of Plympton is already rapidly expanding. Within twenty years it will be little more than a dormitory suburb of Plymouth, although locals will still quote the verse that holds that, in the Middle Ages,

Plympton was a borough town
When Plymouth was a fuzzy down.

The avenue of trees leads from a folly near Plymbridge Road, known as 'Triumphal Arch', all the way across the valley to Saltram House, home of the Parkers, the Earls of Morley, who moved there from Boringdon Hall. The arch was built to celebrate Great Britain's part in rescuing Europe from Napoleon and ensuring her own freedom at Trafalgar in 1805 and, ten years later, at Waterloo.

But in my cousin John's photograph there is a contrast with the steadiness of Dad's touch on my shoulders (Plate 11). It is the look on his face. What does it show? Worry? Uncertainty? Confusion? Whatever it is, there seems for the moment to be no shadow of it in Mum's expression, or in Ralf's, preoccupied with the giant mushroom in his hands. But perhaps I also look confused or quizzical. What is happening? Time will tell.

2
Chromosome 4
gene IT15

IT ALL BEGAN with Chromosome 4.

It always begins with Chromosome 4 gene IT15, a few specks of matter.

Sometimes, perhaps in sixty cases in a million, a fault is there. No one knows why. It just happens. The coding of the gene is extended a little, and that unnecessary extension is the cause of it all.

If the fault is there in the gene, then it leads to Huntington's chorea, Huntington's disease, usually in middle age.

It is what they used to call St Vitus' dance. *Chorea* means dance.

That's what happened in Dad's family. No one suspected it would happen.

If a person has the Huntington's gene, each sperm or egg contains two copies of Chromosome 4, gene IT15, one inherited from each parent; one normal and one faulty.

So, if such a person marries a person without Huntington's, and they then have a child, the child inherits a normal Chromosome 4 gene IT15 from the healthy parent but *either* a normal *or* a faulty gene from the parent with Huntington's.

In this way, a child of someone with the disease has a 50-50 chance of inheriting it. It is as simple as that: a 50-50 chance, the toss of a coin. It never skips a generation.

Either way, the child's fate is sealed.

Inherit the faulty gene, and you develop Huntington's. Or inherit the healthy gene, and you see your afflicted parent disappear, fragment before your eyes, and die of the disease; and then, unless you take a genetic test to see if the coin landed heads or tails in your own case, you live with that question unresolved for the rest of your life.

This is the story of how this disease affected Dad and his six sisters, the lives of everyone in his family. Huntington's is a disease of families as well as those who die of it.

It is the story of how they responded. It is as true as I can make it. Huntington's is still at work.

3

Florence Louisa and William

DAD WAS BORN in December 1901. He was the only son and the eldest child in the family. My Auntie Florrie, named after their mother, and the first of six sisters, was born a couple of years later. It was she who helped me to build up a picture of their life. I had been too young to take it all in properly when Dad was alive and well.

Auntie Florrie lived longer than the others and she was in good health almost to the end of her ninety-one years. In the 1980s and 1990s, as her life began to draw to a close, I used to travel down from London and visit her at Heamoor, only a hundred yards from Wesley Rock Chapel, where her parents were married. She lived in Wesley Street quietly with her youngest son, Coulson, in the well-built stone cottage that had come to her through her late husband, Charlie Paul. The Pauls had lived in the area for generations and the family's building firm had built the houses in that street late in the nineteenth century when, for a while, they were quite prosperous.

The sleeper from Paddington used to arrive at Penzance, at the end of the line, by about 8 o'clock. I would take a taxi and call in at a florist's shop to buy Auntie Florrie some freesias or anemones, and then, at no. 3 Wesley Street, she would give me a Cornish welcome and a grand breakfast of eggs and bacon and fried bread. Wearing a long apron over her cardigan and tweed skirt, she wielded her frying pan and fish-slice boisterously. She stood straight for her years. Her thick grey hair, her quiet smile, the shape and angle of her forehead and her dark, blue-grey eyes spoke to me of Dad, and I dare to believe that, in some way, I made his presence real for her.

9

Then we got down to business. Sitting at the kitchen table by the fireplace with paper and pencil, we would roam over what she remembered of her family's life. Coulson would stay on the edge of this, listening with interest to parts of the conversation, never making his presence and keen attention too obvious to his mother, moving in and out of the kitchen, sometimes going for a while into the back yard where red pelargoniums and other bright flowers grew strongly in carefully tended pots.

Once Coulson told me that, whenever he asked Auntie Florrie about the family, she used to say, *'Why do you want to know about that? You never know what you might find out if you ask questions like that!'* But with me she was always at ease and open in talking about the family. She seemed to delight in passing on to her only brother's elder son what she, among the living, alone now knew. Often she seemed to sense in advance the questions I was about to ask, particularly when the matter was sad, and then we would shed a few quiet tears together, but just as often we laughed at stories from the past. Perhaps we both knew that time was short; the years were running out. We were talking just in the nick of time.

At the end of the morning I would gather all my papers into my briefcase and Auntie Florrie would take out of the oven three of her golden-brown Cornish pasties. No one made better pasties, my mother told me. Coulson would join us. And then I would be away, usually for another twelve months, on the train heading for London.

I owe Auntie Florrie so much.

Like Auntie Florrie, Dad loved and revered their mother, Florence Louisa and their father, William. Mum also told me that Dad's mother had been a wonderful woman to whom he was devoted, but if Dad himself said anything to me about them, it must have been when I was too young to take it in.

William and his father John Hocking Symons, and their ancestors, had lived in the far west of Cornwall and worked the seas around Newlyn, or laboured on the land there, for all of the nineteenth century, and probably for many centuries before that. It is a surprise that, by contrast, John Hocking's wife Peace and her family came from the industrial towns of Batley and Dewsbury, just south of Bradford and Leeds in Yorkshire.

How John Hocking and Peace met, I do not know. Peace's parents may have originated in Hull, Whitby or Scarborough, or one of the other fishing towns and villages on the east coast of England, and worked there until the industrial revolution drew them to the West Riding of Yorkshire. Probably, in the mid-1860s, John Hocking visited the east coast and for a while worked on the fishing fleet at Scarborough – that is what his grandchildren believed – when the fishing was bad in the western seas off Newlyn. He moved inland to Mirfield and married, but his first wife died only two years later of tuberculosis, 'phthisis' in the medical language of those days. They had no children.

John Hocking stayed on in the Mirfield area, working at an iron foundry, and in due course he met Peace there. They married in 1875. Their first son Frank was born in Mirfield in West Yorkshire in 1876, but, by the time that William, the second son and my grandfather, was born in 1879 they were living in Penzance. In 1881 the Census records that the family, by then with a third son, Ernest, was living in Jack Lane in Newlyn.

Twenty years later at the time of the Census in April 1901 John Hocking was still working as a fisherman, but he was no longer fit. His three eldest sons, by then twenty-four, twenty-two and twenty years old, were all fishermen, and perhaps they joked with him that he had been at sea too long – even on land he seemed to keep his sea legs and to sway unsteadily. That was not because of drink. The Wesleyan, teetotal influence was strong in Newlyn. John Hocking and Peace and their family were Methodists. Perhaps the young men thought that the same thing would happen to them if they stayed at sea for too long. Had not their grandfather, Frank, ended up like that, working as a labourer on the land at the end of his life, after so many years at sea, until he died of malaria? So, like his father before him, John Hocking sorted out and cleaned the nets on the quayside and left the fishing to his three eldest boys. The youngest, Alfred, was only twelve years old, in his last year at school. Alfred was the last child in John Hocking and Peace's family.

By the turn of 1901, when Queen Victoria died and, in the last moments of her life, sensed the presence of her consort Prince Albert and called out to him on her way to be reunited with him after so many years of widowhood, William had met Florence Louisa. Later that year they married.

Florence Louisa's background was much less settled than William's. The marriage certificate in August 1901 gives her full name as Florence Louisa Groves. She was twenty years old. No father is mentioned in her line in the certificate, which just reads: 'Florence Louisa Groves.

20 years. Spinster. Residence at time of marriage – Marine Place, Penzance.' No 'rank or profession' is listed.

The 1901 Census shows that in April that year Florence Louisa was living alone at 26 Back Marine Terrace. It states that she was nineteen years old and was working as a charwoman, but, seeing the family photograph taken in November 1914, someone said to me, *'You can see that she was a lady.'* I can. Like Dad, I too have come to love Florence Louisa for what she did and suffered; for what she was – for her loyalty and courage. Perhaps you will see what I mean.

Florence Louisa and William both signed the register after their wedding service, but John Hocking Symons, William's father (profession: 'Fisherman retired'), one of the witnesses of their marriage, made his mark with a cross. His hand was now too unsteady to write. Twenty-six years earlier he had been able to write his signature on his own marriage certificate, whereas Peace had made her mark with a cross.

Towards the end of her life Auntie Florrie told me that it was because she was born on the day of the Helston Floral or 'Furry' Dance, – 8th May – that their mother was named Florence. Auntie Florrie also told me that Florence Louisa's mother was called Susie and that she died not long before her daughter's wedding. She was giving me clues so that, one day, I could find out more for myself.

Although memories in a family of coincidences like that often prove to be good evidence and a sound guide, there is no trace of a birth certificate for Florence Louisa Groves. All my efforts to find her birth in the records, civil, church and chapel, proved futile.

One day I explained the problem to the supervisor of the local registry in Penzance. After searching the original documents, she told me that, although there was no birth recorded for a Florence Louisa *Groves* on 8th May 1881, there was a Florence Louisa *Saundry*, born to a Susan Saundry in Penzance (Madron) on that day. And then there was a death certificate for a Susan Saundry on the 10th of February 1900, reported by an 'F. Saundry' of 3 Marine Place.

The likelihood that this 'F. Saundry' was the same person as Florence Louisa Groves, who married William Symons, is borne out by an entry in the 1891 Census. This shows, lodging in two rooms at 9 Cornwall Terrace, Penzance (close to Marine Place): 'Susan S. Groves, lodger, single, 41 years, retired housekeeper, b. St. Columb Minor; and Florence L. Groves, daughter 9, scholar, b. Penzance.'

The dry, dusty documents make it all too clear that Florence Louisa had a hard start in life. For, according to the birth certificate, she was born in Penzance Union Workhouse at Madron. Dad's beloved mother was born in a workhouse.

How this happened, it is impossible to say. The records now available show that Susan Saundry was born into a family of farm labourers and fishermen who seem to have lived in the Padstow area on the north coast of Cornwall throughout the nineteenth century. The seas and currents there are treacherous, and the land is not rich, for all the area's beauty and its attractions now as a holiday coastline.

What took Susan Saundry to Penzance is also not clear. Another puzzle is that she is said, in her death certificate, to be the widow of James Saundry, a journeyman basket-maker. Perhaps Susan married someone, possibly a cousin, with the same surname, and his work took her the thirty miles southwest from Padstow to Penzance where the fishing, especially at Newlyn, was on a bigger scale. Perhaps he died just after Florence Louisa's conception, leaving Susan his widow destitute and so far from the home of the rest of her family that her only refuge was the Penzance Union Workhouse. Certainly, the 1881 Census lists her as a 'pauper'; but it also reckons her 'unmarried'. Perhaps that is a mistake for 'widow'. After all, the census enumerator had to list 135 inmates and 11 officers at the workhouse. Such a mistake would have been easily made. But of James Saundry himself, there is no death certificate in the preceding period, nor is there any other likely trace in the records. He appears on his widow's death certificate, and that is all.

After the death of her mother Susan in 1900, Florence Louisa seems to have been alone in the world. She worked as a charwoman and lived in a tiny room at the back of Marine Terrace on Penzance promenade, where the sea was sometimes so wild during winter storms that the waves washed into the houses. A remote cousin, whom Auntie Florrie, at the end of her life, would remember faintly as 'Uncle Phillip', seems to have helped Susan, and perhaps, after her mother's death, Florence Louisa herself. This may have been Phillip Groves, who with his wife Georgeina and their children, lived in Penzance around the corner from Susan and Florence Louisa in 1891, when the Census shows the two of them using the surname Groves. But Phillip and his family disappeared from Florence Louisa's life. Somehow, she survived on her own at 26 Back Marine Terrace, later demolished in slum clearance.

So on 4th August 1901 Florence Louisa Groves and William Symons were married in the chapel at Heamoor. The chapel had been built on the site of the Rock on which Wesley used to stand and preach the gospel in the fields a hundred and fifty years earlier. Wesley's work in the area led to many people being converted to a deep Christian faith, and they in their turn exerted a dramatic and beneficial influence on the morals and way of life in Penzance and Newlyn, and generally in west Cornwall for many years to come.

After the wedding William and Florence Louisa went to live at no. 3 Marine Place. On 11th December Dad was born there.

The family lived for a little longer in Penzance, but soon William and Florence Louisa moved to Newlyn where they spent the rest of their short lives, living first at Paul Hill, then Duke Street, and then Paul Hill again.

Finally in 1913 they settled at no. 4 Jack Lane. This was to be the family home for more than twenty years, until it and several other cottages in the row were, falsely and humiliatingly, declared 'unfit to live in' and, decades later, demolished.

Dad's six sisters were born between his arrival at the end of 1901 and the outbreak of the Great War in August 1914: Florrie in 1903, Suzie in 1905, Nora in 1908, Rene in 1910, Clara in 1911, and Kathleen in 1913.

The family was complete.

Newlyn before 1914

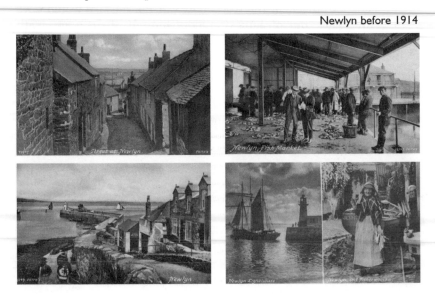

4
'On Chorea'

IN 1907 Dad's grandfather, John Hocking, died. On the death certificate the doctor, A. Herbert Hart, MD, stated that the cause of death
was 'chorea exhaustion' as well as heart failure. There was more to
his unsteadiness than his sons' jokes about sea legs on land had
acknowledged.

What was his widow, Peace, to make of that obscure term? Perhaps
she had heard of St Vitus' dance. With its static population and the
risk of inbreeding, west Cornwall, like other remote areas, was prey to
hereditary illnesses.

And what did Dr Hart know, let alone tell Peace, about her husband's
condition? How could a physician in west Cornwall in 1907 have read
the 1872 issue of the *Medical and Social Reporter* of Philadelphia, in the
United States, in which George Huntington published the scientific
paper entitled 'On Chorea' that would for ever associate his name with
this disease?

After all, John Hocking had lived to sixty-six years, a good age by the
standards of the time and place and occupation. Two of his sons would
die much younger. The day-to-day struggle to make a living was enough
to exhaust all the energies of his sons and their families. John Hocking
was lucky, in a way, to have reached sixty-six years.

What impact the sight of his grandfather's illness and death had on
Dad, I cannot tell. He was in only his sixth year when John Hocking
died, and by then Peace was probably protecting, or screening, John
Hocking from everyone, even from his young grandchildren. Dad told
his younger sisters of his love for his grandmother and of her care for
him as a little boy. He recalled how, each June, she used to hang elder-
flower blossoms from a beam in the kitchen 'to keep away the flies', but

he never mentioned his grandfather. Perhaps he could not remember him at all. The only thing that Auntie Florrie could remember was that she had heard from someone that their grandfather was *shaky* at the end of his life.

So John Hocking probably faded gradually from his grandchildren's life, leaving at most a hazy image in Dad's memory of an ailing grandfather, who died just after he had started to attend Wesley School in The Fradgan, in Newlyn.

In the years in which Dad and his sisters were born, William, their father was earning his living in various ways. His main occupation was with the fishing fleet in Newlyn Bay, but his wages from that work were tiny and unpredictable. He also did general labouring and worked on the local farms. In addition, he joined the Royal Naval Reserve, and in 1910 and 1913 served in the Merchant Marine.

From her early years Florence Louisa suffered from poor health. She was often ill, especially after an operation of some sort on her neck. *'Our mother was never well,'* Auntie Florrie told me. She made it a habit to eat as little as she could in order to have enough to feed the children. When she made Cornish pasties, she used to put all the meat in those that she cooked for her family, while in her own she would put just a scrap of bone to make a little juice to give flavour to the potato and swede. It was a *'bone pasty'*, Auntie Florrie said, after eighty years still in awe of her mother's loving kindness.

From his early years, as a schoolboy, Dad sometimes worked at the baker's shop at the top of Jack Lane (its successor, Eddy's Bakery, was there, selling pasties and bread and Cornish saffron cake, until 2007), and at other times he delivered newspapers.

About thirty yards along Jack Lane from where William, Florence Louisa and their growing family were living, William's brother Frank occupied another tiny cottage. Frank was two years older than William and, like him, was a fisherman. Frank never married. By and large, the men in the Symons family married in their thirties, and by that age Frank was already ill.

In the summer of 1910, when King Edward VII died and was succeeded by King George V, Dad was eight years old, and three of his sisters had been born. Already the first signs of their Uncle Frank's illness were visible, reminding the adults in the family of John Hocking's wasting illness and death, and slowly extending over the family the shadow of what was to befall Frank.

Then, only three months after the outbreak of war, William died. He had been serving as an Able Seaman on HMS Alexandra, and was involved in an early action against the Imperial German fleet. As a result of the engagement, many of the crew found themselves in the sea for some time. William's heart came under severe stress, and finally, after four days in the Royal Naval Hospital at Stonehouse in Devonport, gave way to acute pericarditis and the collapse of the mitral valve.

William was thirty six years old. He died before the Huntington's gene, which unwittingly he had passed on to his son and two of his daughters, could begin to do its work in him.

At the end of 1914 Frank moved house. The records are not clear. He may have settled with Florence Louisa and her children after William's death, but more probably he joined his mother, Peace, who was by then living with his brother Alfred and his wife Maud and their two daughters, in yet another cottage in Jack Lane.

The other remaining Symons brother, Ernest, probably also lived nearby. He and his wife Ellen, in the course of time, produced a family of eight children.

$$Q$$

Among William's generation of the family, Maud, Alfred's wife, lived longest. She was still alive when I married in 1971. By then doctors knew more about Huntington's disease. I wanted to find out what I could about its effects on my family and the prospects for my future and that of my wife-to-be.

At my request, but reluctantly, Mum asked Florrie about it. I suggested that great-aunt Maud might know more than anyone else and be able to help.

The time was not right. Auntie Florrie was not yet able to speak openly about it all. She seemed to resent my questions. In her letter to Mum she wrote, 'Jack is a wonderful person and the boys need to be proud of him, as I'm sure Jack is proud of his family.' I did not need to be told this.

Auntie Florrie's wounds were still raw, too tender to touch. That is the way it often is for families with Huntington's disease. It is a disease of families, not just individuals, but its effects on families can sometimes be overcome.

Fifteen years later I began my visits to see Auntie Florrie at Heamoor and could try to unravel the truth with her. By then, the time was right.

Much later, after her death, cousin Coulson told me that the long, quiet talks I had with her in her last years had helped Auntie Florrie and him, as well as me, to come to terms with our family's past. The three of us were lucky to have those days together; they gave us joy. Dad would have been pleased. It was as if he was there with us, bringing us his gift of peace.

5

'One and All'*

WILLIAM'S DEATH and Florence Louisa's poor health almost snuffed out Dad's family. In the photograph of the eight of them, in mourning in November 1914, the children are gathered close together around their mother to comfort and protect her and each other.

At first the local authorities wanted to separate the children – aged between one and thirteen years – and put them out to be fostered. It would have broken up the family. Somehow, Florence Louisa managed to prevent this and to bring them up together.

Seventy-five years later, Auntie Florrie told me that it was the 'tanners'† that Dad earned that saved the family. Florence Louisa's devotion, Dad's 'tanners', the common sense of the six girls, and the shrewd, watchful eye of Peace somehow kept them together. As a war widow, Florence Louisa received a tiny pension from the Royal Navy.

Somehow they all kept together and survived, and successfully brought up the younger sisters. Jack, Florrie and Suzie, the three eldest children, shared the work among themselves. Jack earned what he could; Florrie and Suzie took care of their mother, Jack and their younger sisters.

Dad left school in 1915, soon after his thirteenth birthday. You can see his intelligence and longing to learn in the school photograph that Florence Louisa and his sisters gave him as a birthday present when he left school (Plate 3). Dad is standing, already tall, next to the young teacher. On the back is the only example of Florence Louisa's writing,

---

* This, the motto of Cornwall, is *'onnen hag ol'* in the Cornish language.
† A tanner was sixpence in £.s.d, pounds, shillings and pence, abolished in 1971, 2½ pence in 'new money'.

in pencil: *'To our darling Jack from Mother and Sisters wishing you many happy returns of your birthday'* (followed by 24 kisses).

Dad went to work for Dick Bath, the coal merchant, at Newlyn harbour, 'heaving coal', as Auntie Florrie put it. He later drove the firm's horse and cart to make coal deliveries. He stayed there for almost three years.

In 1916 Florrie went 'into service'. At first, she worked locally at Faugan farm, walking there and back every day from Jack Lane. She remembered the grandmother of the family at the farm making cream by hand and churning butter; the son of the family was away at the War in France.

When Suzie in turn left school in 1918 and was able to do more at home, Florrie could move to better paid work. She visited Peace's family, the Crawshaws, in Yorkshire, and they put her in touch with a doctor in Hertfordshire for whose family she worked, at Totteridge or Potter's Bar, for a few months. But after that short absence from Cornwall, she returned home and went to live and work in the village of Pendeen. There she worked for the family of Captain Hitchens, who at one time had been skipper of the steamer *Scillonian*, in those days the only regular link between Penzance and the Isles of Scilly. Captain Hitchens had by now been appointed to run the lighthouse, Pendeen Watch, built on the headland there in 1910. There had been many shipwrecks over the years on that wild coast, north of Land's End and St Just. Florrie managed to get home once a week, and, like Jack, shared her wages with the family. She remained in service at Pendeen until her marriage in 1926.

These years brought the three eldest children very close to one another, especially Jack and Suzie, who were living at home and caring for the family. As Florence Louisa's health worsened – she was suffering from tuberculosis – she started to spend much of her time, and to sleep by night, in a little wooden shed on the far side of the back yard of their cottage. Perhaps this helped her breathing, but she did it mainly in order to protect her children from the disease. At that time the cause of tuberculosis was unknown and there was no cure. She taught Suzie to cook. Because of her care, none of the children developed TB, and all of them, except Kathleen, the youngest, were fit. Kathleen suffered, from her early years, from rheumatic fever.

Life was a struggle. At the end of the Great War conditions had not eased in Great Britain. Prices continued to rise rapidly in 1919 and the early 1920s. There was an uneasy spirit of turmoil fermenting in the country. The government was hard pressed to maintain social peace and security. It introduced some political and social reforms, but the mood did not improve much.

In 1919 the Prime Minister, David Lloyd George, spoke some words in the House of Commons about the crisis that even caught the attention of Lenin and the Bolsheviks in Moscow, giving them hope in the middle of the Russian civil war when power seemed, for a while, to be slipping away from them. In a speech that was quoted in history textbooks in Russia, even after the end of Communism there in 1991, Lloyd George was reported to have said:

> All Europe is seething with the fever of revolution ... Everywhere there is, not so much a spirit of dissatisfaction, as of anger or vengeance among working men, even open fury against the conditions which they experienced before the War. The popular masses of Europe, from one end to the other, put in question the future of all the existing order, all the current political, social and economic structures of society. (My translation)

In 1920, when Lloyd George's government wished to support Poland against Soviet Russia after the Red Army, on Lenin's orders, had marched on Warsaw, later to be defeated by the Poles, the British trade unions forced Lloyd George to back down and to withdraw the government's ultimatum to Russia. This experience so encouraged Lenin in his conviction that world revolution was on its way that he said:

> We have reached the English proletariat ... Political forces in England are at that stage of development that we Bolsheviks enjoyed in Russia after February 1917 when the Soviets were compelled to control each step of the bourgeois government ... It is a dyarchy.

Although the political and economic crisis in Great Britain gradually eased, it remained a struggle for Florence Louisa's family, like so many others, to survive.

Dad sensed that he had to do something decisive for himself and his family. At first Florence Louisa was upset and worried when he told her what he had in mind. She had lost her husband to the Germans in the War and now, when Ireland and the Continent were still in chaos and some countries were suffering revolution and fresh bloodshed, her only son planned to join the Army.

But Dad, Florrie and Suzie had worked out together what needed to be done. The family needed more money and their mother more medicines and better food. Dad said, *'I won't spend the rest of my life heaving coal for Dick Bath for a few shillings a week.'* Only the Army offered him clothing, regular food, a steady wage and enough to send something home. It was also a great attraction for him that it would give him more education.

In the end Florence Louisa accepted the good sense of what her three eldest children had decided. On St George's day, 23rd April 1919, Dad joined the British Army. He signed on as a private soldier with the Duke of Cornwall's Light Infantry (DCLI) at Bodmin. His Army service book lists his trade on joining up as 'horse-driver'.

For the next three years Dad served with the second battalion of the DCLI in Ireland, at Ballyshannon in County Donegal and in County Clare in the war against the Irish Republican Army. It was a bitter war and a hard life. At that time he said, *'If anyone from Newlyn says that he wants to join the Army, take him to the harbour and throw him in.'*

Early in 1921 Florence Louisa became critically ill. Dad was given compassionate leave to visit her in Cornwall. He arrived home on a Thursday and had a long talk with his mother. The next day, 17th February, Florence Louisa died peacefully in his arms.

In addition to her *'generalised tuberculosis'*, Dr Ronald Thornhill, MB, ChB certified that the cause of death was *'inanition'*, wasting away or starvation caused by the poverty of their life, the effects of the long German blockade of Great Britain, and the economic turmoil arising from the Great War and its aftermath.

A month after Florence Louisa's death, Uncle Frank's life also came to its end. He died not far from his home in a small hospital or nursing home at Mount View on Paul Hill, from where St Michael's Mount and Marazion could be seen across the bay to the northeast. The cause of his death is recorded by Dr R.C. Lawry, MRCS as *'chorea gravidum'* and exhaustion. Perhaps his Uncle Frank's ungainly, choreic movements reminded Dad how his grandfather's life had ended when he had been five years old. Frank's passing was registered by Maud, the wife of his brother Alfred; she had nursed him for years. He was only forty four years old.

In December 1921 the Irish Free State was set up. After a terrible civil war, comparative calm came to Ireland. Many regiments of the British Army, including Dad's, were withdrawn from the island.

The only thing that Jack and his sisters could do was to soldier on in their different ways.

Together, Florence Louisa and William, against the odds, had created a family strong enough to stand the test of time.

Bone Pasty

They call it mother love:
    For me it means bone pasty.

It means a wooden shack
    The far side of the yard
To sleep and breathe and keep
    The children TB-free.
It means Dad's heaving coal
    On Newlyn quay;
The tanners that he earned and placed upon
    The kitchen table.
It means his Mum – my granny – mixing flour
    And water; slicing swede
And spreading scraps of gristly beef;
    And then, in hers, no meat –
A bone, for juice, – a bone:
    A phantom of a Cornish pasty.

They speak of mother love:
    For me it means bone pasty.

Florence Louisa Groves
8th May 1881 to 17th February 1921
R.I.P.

Beatus vir: Blessed is the man ...
(Psalm 1, verse 1)

You could see it as a blessed and a timely
    Death, at thirty-six.

The naval hospital at Devonport
    Provided drugs and care,
And at the end a decent grave –
    Two other ratings share the stone;
And, for his widow and their son
    And their six girls, a pension
For a while, and a name revered
    For all their days, with no
Collapse of mind and will,
    No horror in the eyes
Of those he loved, who loved him still.

An early death is often best,
    For those with eyes to see.

William Symons, RN
14th June 1878 to 5th November 1914
R.I.P.

6

India

THE END of the emergency in Ireland led to the withdrawal of Dad's regiment to England. The first battalion of the Duke of Cornwall's Light Infantry was to be sent to serve in India, where it would remain for many years, and Dad decided to transfer from the second battalion and go there with it.

Florence Louisa's tiny income from her widow's pension from the Royal Navy had died with her. By volunteering to go to India Dad would increase his pay a little, and would receive many other opportunities. He would be able to save and to send more money back home to help Florrie and Suzie to support their younger sisters.

This move gave Dad opportunities for travel and for learning a foreign language that, as a child, he could not have imagined would come to him. He came to love the Indians and India. He learnt so much about the world and its ways in the twenty-five years that he spent there.

His love of England and of India went hand in hand. He sometimes used to quote Kipling's line to me:

And what should they know of England who only England know?

From the bitter-sweet tone in which he voiced that line, I sensed that he felt that many of the people who governed Great Britain in later years undervalued the treasure that had come their way. They had not lived abroad for any length of time and were curiously ignorant of the wider world. Later I understood that, in many cases, they had come to power in Church and State only because so many of the best people of Dad's generation and their predecessors and successors had gone abroad, in their twenties, and stayed on to serve the peoples of the Empire.

Q

On a Saturday morning in early December 1989 I am sitting at the kitchen table, after breakfast, with Auntie Florrie in Wesley Street. We have been working hard on the family tree and the story of the early days.

Auntie Florrie is still fit and well, so alert and interested, and so like Dad that I feel him there with us. She falls silent for a while at the end of our long talk. She stirs herself and suddenly flushes slightly – I have never before seen her colour change in this way – and then looks me straight in the eye, with Dad's calm grey eyes.

'*They said that he was the best boy ever to leave Newlyn*', she says. And then I know that it is true, as her sons and daughter told me, that Dad was, and remained, a hero for his sisters.*

Q

Dad found help and support at home when he was thinking about going to India. Florrie and Suzie encouraged him to go, although they all knew that it would be 1929 at the earliest before they would see one another again. A private soldier serving in India received home leave once every seven years, but life in the army there would give him much more of a chance to make something of his life than he would have if he left the army and returned to Newlyn.

Mr Phelps, the vicar of St Peter's church, also helped Dad to weigh everything up and to take the decision. Auntie Florrie remembered Dad going to talk to him about it.

The vicar knew the family well. After their father died, Florence Louisa's health grew worse and worse and she was house-bound. The seven children used to go on their own to Chapel and Church, turn and turn about, in the morning and evening. If they went to the Methodist chapel on Paul Hill† in the morning, in the evening they would go to

---

* Many young people had found it necessary to leave Newlyn to find a future. It was a well-known local stonemason, Arnold Snell, who reported to Auntie Florrie the feeling there that Dad had been the best boy to leave the little town. Mr Snell worked on the restoration of St Paul's Cathedral in the City of London after the Second World War.

† The chapel is an elegant early-nineteenth-century building, which is still standing. It was partly closed by 11 December 2001, when I visited it on the one hundredth anniversary of Dad's birth, with only a small meeting room open for worship; it was later closed completely and was nominated in 2006 as one of the buildings in England most deserving to be fully restored.

St Peter's church in The Coombe, built in the middle of Queen Victoria's reign.

Dad arrived in India in April 1922.

Over the next few years, five of his sisters married: Suzie in 1925, Florrie in 1926, Rene in 1929 and Clara and Nora in 1930. Dad, Clara and their youngest sister, Kathleen, were three who developed Huntington's.*

Just as a fragile stability was beginning to establish itself, Suzie died in childbirth in October 1925 at West Cornwall Infirmary, Penzance. It was a completely unnecessary death, Auntie Florrie told me. The death certificate records:

Childbirth post partum haemorrhage and shock ... No P[ost] M[ortem].

Suzie's baby died, too. The doctor who signed the certificate deployed an impressive array of initials after his name: 'S.C. Mitchell MB, BCh, BA Obstetrics Trinity College, Dublin'. The qualification in obstetrics had, sadly, done nothing to save Suzie or her baby.

By now Dad was well into his fourth year in India. Florrie wrote to give him the terrible news. Dad replied that he would arrange to come back to England and transfer to the second battalion of the DCLI serving there.

Florrie and the others wrote back to him immediately. They pressed him to stay on in India, and insisted that, together, they would cope. Not only was the pay better in India, which helped them all, but also Dad was beginning to flourish there. He was making a success of army life, and he was enjoying it much more than he had in England or Ireland.

As his sisters married and set up home and began to bring up their children, Dad's letters came to them with an amazing series of post-marks, which intrigued and lodged in the memories of his young nephews and nieces.

In those years the Duke of Cornwall's Light Infantry served at Chakrata in the hills between Derha Dun and Simla in 1922 to 1923; at Lucknow near Cawnpore (now Kanpur) from 1923 to 1927; and at Lebong in Darjeeling/Bengal from 1928 to 1930. From time to time Dad

---

* Clara and her husband, Charlie, had a son and four daughters; of the five children, only one, a daughter, has not developed Huntington's. Kathleen, though beautiful and gentle, always suffered from poor health; she never married.

was able to travel a little. He laid down vivid memories of the Rivers Ganges and Jumna, and of Mt Kanchenjunga, the third highest mountain in the world, and above all of the patient nature of the Indian people, prepared to wait another week at the roadside if they missed this week's bus. He admired them for it.

In the 1930s the regiment served for four years, from 1931 to 1934, at Bareilly, an important railhead and centre on the plain in the north of the United Provinces, not far from the border with Nepal. It moved to Razmak, on the North West frontier with Afghanistan in October 1934 and served there for a year until October 1935. The next postings for the regiment were to Dinapore, near Patna on the River Ganges (now called the Ganga) from 1935 to 1937; and to Lahore in January 1938, in what is now Pakistan. But, by 1930, Dad had been detached from the DCLI for non-regimental service and had been posted to the Indian Army's Infantry School at Pachmarhi in the Central Provinces.

On a bookcase in my dining-room stand three silver cups. Dad bought a set of these bookcases for my brother and me when we were at primary school and were enthusiastically beginning to read.

The silver cups go back to the early years of Dad's time in India. One of them is dated '1927'. It commemorates the first prize won by Dad's tug-of-war team at the annual athletic sports of 19th Indian Infantry Brigade, of which the first battalion of the DCLI formed a part.

There is a photograph, too, of the team which won the trophy in four successive years. The caption records 'Pte Symons' as a member of the

110 stone tug-of-war team.
Winners of the Lucknow Brigade Cups and Medals
1924, 1925, 1926 and 1927.

In front of the ten men of the team, their coach (a company sergeant-major) and their commanding officer, Col. Goldsmith, is coiled the rope, perhaps two inches in diameter, and near it are displayed the winning team's cup and shield, and on either side of them, in two rows, the smaller cups presented to the team members.

But of course it is the image of Dad which holds my attention. How fit and well he looks, how completely at ease, how flourishing! Everything was going well for him in India, and for his remaining five sisters and their young families at Home. (Dad is standing third from the left, behind Colonel Goldsmith.)

Dad is standing third from the left, behind Colonel Goldsmith

None of Dad's many letters Home from those years survives, but one document does, much folded and a little worn. Dad kept it safe in his wallet for nearly fifty years, to the end of his life. The paper is marked in pencil, in Dad's own hand: '5430269 Pte W. Symons, A Coy, 1/DCLI Chakrata, India, 12/8/23'. It reads:

Personal Address to All Ranks by
Lt. Col. H.D. Goldsmith DSO
Commanding
1st Battalion, The Duke of Cornwall's Light Infantry.

On being gazetted to command the Battalion with which I have been connected for nearly 26 years, my chief feeling is one of pride at being at the head of a unit with such a long and distinguished record both in peace and war.

I wish to remind all ranks, however, that we must not be content to live on our past records, however glorious, and am confident that I can count on the loyal and whole-hearted cooperation of one and all to maintain and, if possible, to enhance the standard of soldierly excellence the Battalion has borne in the past.

We are shortly moving to a station, which is indelibly associated with our name. In and about Lucknow are the graves of some 400 Officers, NCOs, and men who gave their lives in the successful Defence of the Residency.*

This success was due not to any one individual but to the stubborn courage, determination and devotion to duty of all ranks.

Wherever the Regiment has served, it has always earned a name for good sportsmanship, and good conduct, both in and out of barracks.

One of the best tributes ever paid to these traditions was in the farewell address to the Battalion in 1912 by the inhabitants of Gravesend, in which it was said that, by their conduct there, the Battalion had earned the name of a Regiment of Gentlemen.

I feel sure that everyone of you will make it a point of honour to live up to that title, and to emulate the example set by our forefathers of the 32nd Foot in the past.   CHAKRATA 11.8.23   H.D. GOLDSMITH, LT-COLONEL

This strong sense of purpose and identity, of duty and principles, openly expressed, gave those who came to share it a clear and honourable meaning for their lives. There truly was an ideal of a 'regiment of gentlemen' in the Battalion. There was a power in it. In Dad's case, this shared ideal was built on the Christian influence of his family and all that they had learnt together from his earliest years. These principles shaped his life. They helped him, and through him enabled his family, to find their way through what lay ahead.

In 1929 Dad became eligible for his first home leave. It was the year in which his sister Rene married Harold at St Peter's, Newlyn. Perhaps Dad was there and was able to give Rene in marriage at St Peter's, but there is no photograph of the wedding; there was no spare money. No one now alive knows what happened when Dad came home in 1929 and how he and his sisters celebrated their time together.

Megan, Rene's daughter, told me, *'They were a close family; they didn't say much about the past.'*

As a result, most of the story of the inch-by-inch improvement in their lives is lost and with it the record of the events accompanying the family weddings and the births of the children of the new generation. One of Nora's sons, among the earliest of my cousins to be born, told me that he remembered his great-grandmother, Peace, showing him what everyone called 'Granny's box' at no. 4 Jack Lane. In the box she kept the

---

* This took place in 1857 during the Indian Mutiny.

Family Bible, some photographs and the family's birth, marriage and death certificates. My cousin remembers seeing the box again in the years after Peace's death in 1931.

Not long after that, the box of family treasures was mislaid, probably when Nora and her family moved house away from the heart of Newlyn, near the harbour, where they had lived for so many years. The move was not of their choice. In the second half of the 1930s some of the houses in Jack Lane were designated for slum clearance. The labelling of the cottages as 'slums' provoked so much outrage among the locals that a small squadron of Newlyn's fishing vessels sailed up the English Channel to the River Thames and protested outside the Houses of Parliament. As a result, most of the cottages were reprieved, but no. 4 was not saved.

Nora, Reg and their sons settled in a house on a newly built council estate. In 1940 the condemned cottages, already boarded up, were re-opened for a while and used by some Belgian fishermen who had fled west across the English Channel from the Germans as their army swept into their country. Soon after the War, and ten years after Nora and the family moved out, no. 4 Jack Lane was levelled to the ground. The plot that it had occupied became a car park

'Granny's box' disappeared, and with it any photographs of Dad's home leave in 1929. So much of the story of those early years is now also lost.

7
'Floruit'

DAD RETURNED to India in the autumn of 1929. He settled into his second term of seven years there. Posted away from the first battalion of the Duke of Cornwall's Light Infantry, he was stationed at the Infantry Small Arms School at Pachmarhi in Central India. He served at the School for the rest of his career in the Army. The School was moved a hundred miles or so from there to the north, to Saugor, and expanded soon after the War broke out. Dad played an important role in organising that move. Many hundreds of officers and men, Indian and British, were to pass through the School on its six-week courses in the next few years.

There were about 45,000 British troops in India in late 1929 when Dad began his posting at Pachmarhi. By that time he was an acting sergeant, and in 1932 he was promoted sergeant. On the 2nd of May 1935, 'by order of the Viceroy and Governor-General of India in Council', he was made a warrant-officer, and from that time until 1940 he was the Regimental Quarter-Master Sergeant at Pachmarhi. It was an achievement of which he could be proud.

Dad was keen to learn Urdu properly and to speak it well. In the April and October of 1933 he passed the lower and higher examinations in Urdu at Jubbalpore. He retained a strong and lively interest in languages for the rest of his life. The Army gave him the sixth-form education that he had missed as a boy. He passed his Higher National Certificate examinations, including English language and literature. He read widely. The signatures that he wrote in the books that he bought at that time show the beautiful copperplate hand that he had developed.

Perhaps these were Dad's happiest years. Pachmarhi is set in the Mahadeo hills, at 3,700 feet. There was a glorious climate to enjoy, comfortable for the British and the Indians. The little town and military cantonment were blessed with many tropical trees and beautiful vegetation, and surrounded by an exotic and mysterious landscape, with a river and waterfalls. Dad was doing work that he enjoyed. He had colleagues, British and Indian, whom he liked. The officers liked and respected him. By 1936 his commanding officer listed him as a man who deserved to be commissioned as a regular officer in the Indian Army. He loved the athletics and games, and enjoyed shooting. Above all, he was unbelievably fit.

Twenty-five years after Dad died, when Mum was lying in her hospital bed following a stroke, she said to me, 'How Dad did *love* you two boys!' She had been telling me that we had given him more happiness than anything else; she really believed it, and her mind was clear as she spoke. But by the time my brother and I were starting to attend school Dad was in his fifties and so much sadness was closing in on him, and indeed on all four of us. In the 1930s Dad had enjoyed steady progress and stability in his career, good friends and colleagues, and a healthy outdoor life at Pachmarhi, which Mum sometimes called his 'spiritual home', meaning his favourite place. He always regretted that he could not take her there.

When we were little boys, Dad used to tell us of his adventures from those days: marches and camps and hunts for man-eating tigers in the jungle; sleeping under the stars with his boots as a pillow and 'brushing' his teeth with a few grains of salt on his index finger; slaking his thirst in green pools of stagnant water; staying awake all night, camping on a small platform in the branches of a tree, with a goat's carcase tied to the trunk, waiting for the big game to arrive. On Saturday mornings when there was no school, Ralf and I would perch on each side of Dad on the bed and he would tell us tales of those years.

The Romans and mediaeval scholars used to speak and write of the time of life at which a person 'flourished' – *'floruit'*. They had in mind a conventional age, and they used the term to date their heroes and leaders in relation to each other. For many people, it seems, their *'floruit'* is in the years between thirty-five and forty-five. However much they achieve later, whatever recognition they receive, it is in those years that they seem to bloom, to be most truly themselves.

So it was with Dad, but in a bitterly exaggerated way. I caught sight only of the afterglow of his *'floruit'*. And after a certain stage that twilight, in its turn, faded so quickly and dramatically for reasons we could not fathom at the time. One day, when I was in my teens, I said to my Mother, *'It's a great anxiety to have elderly parents.'* It was a thoughtless and harsh thing to say, and she always carried it in her heart. But, of course, it was the unknown illness from which Dad was by then suffering that, for all the joys we knew at home together, in fact generated anxiety and fear and isolation.

In the last years of Dad's life, as his powers waned so quickly, perhaps some of the happy memories of those years came back to him. Perhaps, deep inside his mind, not everything was lost. That is the hope I nurse.

@

Three faded green report forms tell the story of Dad's *'floruit'*. They show me what manner of man he was before everything was changed by Huntington's.

On those forms, every autumn, the successive commanding officers at Pachmarhi and, after 1939, at Saugor wrote a summary of Dad's work and character. Three pages, from six different officers, cover the eight years' work, from 1932 to 1939. The ink has faded but the writing is clear, and the story is straightforward and brief. Yet each word means so much to me as a clue to what happened in those years, Dad's healthy years, of which I would otherwise know so little. The single page that covered the first ten years of Dad's time in India is missing.

At the time of the first three reports, Dad was a sergeant:

1932: *'A very reliable and trustworthy NCO. Intelligent, conscientious and thorough in all his work.'*

1933: *'In his work in the carpenter's shop and target store he has shown himself adaptable and resourceful. He carries out his very responsible duties with thoroughness and intelligence.'* (The maintenance of the weapons ranges and targets for firing practice was central to the work of the school).

1934: *'His work during the last twelve months has amply confirmed the estimate of his capacities that I made in the preceding year,'* wrote the same officer as in 1933.

Then, after Dad's first six months as RQMS, the commanding officer wrote of him:

1935: *'Has carried out his duties as RQMS very satisfactorily. Has plenty of self-reliance and initiative, and takes a keen interest not only in his work but also in all matters connected with the small arms school. In his dealings with the Indian ranks and followers of the school, he has shown tact and firmness. Has passed the Higher Standard Urdu.'*

Soon after he was appointed RQMS, Dad began to prepare for his second leave in England. With his higher rate of pay, he increased his savings. He began to buy National Savings certificates, to be redeemed, with interest, in five or ten years' time. Perhaps he was already beginning to think of life after he retired from the Army, or even after the British granted India her independence, a topic much discussed there and in Parliament in the 1930s.

By the middle of that decade British power was threatened on many fronts: in Europe by Germany, and in India by Gandhi (of whom Dad always spoke with respect) and his followers (not all of whom Dad could respect), as well as by the Soviet Union to the North, and by Japan to the East. The exploding economic power, 'anti-colonialism' and immense wealth of the United States made that country, too, a competitor in many fields.

When war came it was clear that, whoever the nominal victor might be, the outcome would not protect British interests, but cause the sun to set on her Empire. The United States and the Soviet Union found themselves joined in an unlikely and foolish campaign against 'colonialism' after they joined the war against Germany in 1941, just as Hitler and Stalin had been united in a malign pact in 1939 at the time when together they dismembered Poland and most of Central and Eastern Europe. The earlier alliance of Hitler and Stalin unleashed the Second World War. The later friendship of Stalin and Roosevelt, and their shared disdain for Churchill as the War progressed, was paradoxically soon to set America and Russia at each other's throats in the Cold War and in their macabre division of the spoils of the *Pax Britannica*.

But war had not yet come and Dad had his leave to look forward to. He opened savings and deposit accounts with Lloyds Bank (with its headquarters at 'Hornby Road, Bombay; incorporated in England'), specially for the trip Home.

He must have been saving everything he could. In February 1936 he was able to transfer £1,000 for use back in Cornwall, leaving £238 in his account in India.

More than sixty years later, as I read his bank books, I remembered that when I was a little boy Dad used to say to me, *'Take care of the pennies and the pounds will take care of themselves.'* Then, when I was older, he once said to me, very thoughtfully, *'It takes a long time to save a thousand pounds.'*

I had no idea then of what he was thinking. Now I saw what those words had really meant. That was the sum that he had saved to take back to Cornwall in 1936. He had done it all for his family. It was for his sisters and then, later, for us that he lived. It was a huge amount of money for a person in his position, and for his family. It is hardly possible to imagine how he had stinted spending on himself in India over the previous years, or how he lavished gifts on the family in Cornwall during his time there that year.

But the most important thing about the family at that time was that none of them was in the grip of Huntington's. Dad's second Home leave took place during a respite for them all.

So, in the summer of 1936, Dad arrived back in Cornwall. He brought with him a new collapsible, accordion-like camera, which years later fascinated me as a little boy. During his time at Home he took many photographs. They show his sisters and their growing families, and him on the beach, wearing one of the modest, long-sleeved swimming costumes of those years. They show the family on walks and making picnics on the Cornish cliffs.

Dad and Kathleen, 1936

Dad also visited Rene and Florrie and their families in the Midlands and in South Devon. He took Florrie's two eldest sons on a railway excursion to Yelverton, and from there on the winding branch-line to Princetown in the heart of Dartmoor. He showed them some of the photographs that he had taken in India, like those that he used to send them with his letters. They captured vivid scenes of his life there: Dad walking across a river with his boots laced together and hanging around his shoulders; standing on a stepping-stone as the water swirls past him; sitting on a canvas chair outside a large tent on an exercise in the jungle; dressed in a light civilian suit in the garden of a bungalow; standing in his long, white umpire's coat in a formal photograph of the Infantry School's cricket team; a night photograph with silvery streams of fire-works; two tiny tiger cubs; a bear cub; photographs of friends on picnics, with a gramophone, and swimming in the river; and several snaps of Dad's Jack Russell terrier, Tuppy.

At the end of the summer he returned to Pachmarhi. A little later, in January 1937, he transferred a further £250 to the Penzance branch of Lloyds for the use of the family in Cornwall, as he settled down for the next seven years in India. As it turned out, the War would mean that he would not see England again for eight years.

Dad's reports in those years show that his work and career went from strength to strength, and that he was marked out for further promotion.

1936: *'An excellent RQMS with an intimate knowledge of his work and all Regulations connected with it. His supervision of both British and Indian ranks is good. His knowledge of Urdu, pleasant and outspoken manner, and his wide grasp of all Quarter-Mastering matters warrant his name being placed upon the list of those recommended for a commission in the Indian Army as Quarter-Masters.'*

1937: the same officer as in 1935 and 1936 wrote, *'He has maintained throughout 1937 a very high standard of efficiency and it is greatly due to his untiring efforts that the Quarter-Mastering branch of the School is so smoothly run. Has a good knowledge of Urdu, and has controlled both the British and Indian staff with tact and firmness. Has a wide knowledge of Regulations and Office work. A keen sportsman.'*

1938: A new commandant of the school reported, *'I entirely concur in the above remarks. He has supervised the Quarter-Mastering branch in an extremely able manner. He is cheerful, resourceful and has plenty of initiative. He has a thorough working command of Urdu, and gets a high standard of efficiency from the staff working under him due to his tact and firmness. He is a warrant-officer in whom I have the utmost trust. I consider him suitable for appointment to the Indian Army as Quarter-Master.'*

1939: A further new commandant wrote, *'He has maintained his high standard. Under his excellent and very efficient supervision the Quarter-Mastering work of the School has proceeded in a smooth and capable manner. He is tactful, always cheerful, and full of resource and initiative. His handling of the staff under him, both British and Indian, is excellent. An excellent type of warrant-officer.'*

Just beneath this report Dad has signed his initials, dating his interview with the commanding officer, '22/8', 22nd August. It was twelve days before the outbreak of the Second World War, the very day that Molotov, Stalin's foreign minister, on behalf of the Soviet Union, and Ribbentrop, on behalf of Hitler, signed their non-aggression pact and, in a secret protocol, agreed to divide Central and Eastern Europe between them. It made the war, already inevitable, infinitely more sinister and destructive.

With the coming of war, the Small Arms School moved from Pachmarhi to Saugor. It took over the training school of the Indian cavalry regiments. Pachmarhi became (and remains) the headquarters of the Indian Army Education Corps. For his part in the move to Saugor, Dad received an additional report:

15 November 1939: *'On the recent reorganisation of the Small Arms School, India, this WO has come to the British Wing at Saugor as RQMS, having previously been employed in a similar capacity at Pachmarhi. I most heartily endorse the remarks of the Commandants of the Pachmarhi Wing, extending over a period of many years. He is a WO of the highest character and his work is excellent in every way.'*

A few months later Dad received his commission as Lieutenant Quartermaster.

He had everything to live for.

8
Commissioned

I REMEMBER Dad's commission. It used to hang in an ebony frame on the wall in Ralf's bedroom. On the wall in my bedroom there was a watercolour of Dad's bungalow in Saugor. Dad and Mum always treated us exactly equally, sharing their treasures between us.

That commission made me feel so proud, but Dad never made any mention of all that he had achieved, having begun life with so little in material terms. Perhaps it was Mum who encouraged him to have it framed.

As he became ill, I remember thinking to myself, *'How is it that Dad who did so much for his country, for all of us, has come to this?'* It was a thought to share with no one, not because there was no one but because there is no way truly to share such a feeling that breaks the heart of a child. Anyone who tells you otherwise has no inkling of what it is like. I loved him and this had happened to him. That was everything.

The commission – at first, an Emergency Commission – came to Dad from the 'King Emperor' George VI, nine months after the declaration of War. On 5th July 1940 he was appointed quartermaster-lieutenant on the list of the First Kumaon Rifles. This was at that time part of the Nineteenth Hyderabad Regiment, which was later renamed the Kumaon Regiment, and is now the Kumaon and Naga Regiment. It is one of the most distinguished regiments in the Indian Army, with twenty or so battalions.

As a boy I used to admire Dad's smart regimental tie, with its green and red stripes, which I now wear at reunions in England. In October 2003 I was honoured to wear it at the Regiment's reunion at its centre at Ranikhet in the Kumaon, not far from India's borders with China and Nepal, and to lay a wreath at the memorial there in honour of those who had served in the Regiment and died in the service of their country. Dad was very close to me there during the silence that we observed.

Dad's service book shows that, when his commission was signed in July 1940, he had served 24 years and 83 days altogether with the DCLI: two years and 319 days in Great Britain and Ireland, and 21 years and 129 days (more than half his life) in India. For all the recommendations going back to the mid 1930s that he should be commissioned, Dad, like many others, finally received this opportunity and responsibility sooner than it might have come, because of the War. He was well prepared.

Ⓒ

Sixty years on from the date of his receiving it, I showed an Indian friend from church Dad's Emergency Commission, confirmed as 'regular' two and a half years later in the document that was to hang in due course on the wall in my brother's bedroom. Maurice had been a Colonel in the Indian Army until his retirement in the 1990s. By an odd coincidence, he was born on the day in 1940 on which Dad was commissioned.

Maurice's eyes began to shine as he read the document. It was, he told me, drafted in more or less the same words as those used, since Independence, by the President of India. Nowadays the words are printed in English on one side of the paper, and given in the officer's vernacular language on the reverse.

Maurice paused on the line referring to the King's *'trust and confidence in your Loyalty, Courage and good Conduct.'* With pride and a burst of joy he said to me, *'It feels exactly like that – the responsibility to behave like that.'*

Dad's feelings, I am sure, were the same. We saw that it was so, even near the end of his life in hospital, when he always stood straight with head held high as the National Anthem was played on the television in the ward.

Ⓒ

It must have been curious for Dad to be commissioned as an officer after serving so long in the ranks and as a warrant officer. After some time as quartermaster he became the administrative officer at the British

Wing, working for the Commandant of the Small Arms School. He helped organise courses for many 'squads' of subalterns sent out from England. As the war gathered pace in the Far East as well as in Europe, a stream of young officers passed through Saugor on training courses, many of them to be sent on to serve in the Middle East or Burma.

These young officers were, for the most part, twenty years younger than Dad, and many of them were accustomed to a life at Home unlike anything that he had experienced there. In *A Shaft of Sunlight*, his memoir of life in India in the 1930s and 1940s, Philip Mason, who worked closely with the Indian Army during his time in the Indian civil service, wrote: 'There was one Major who had risen from the ranks; "Nice young men," he confided in me one day, "but not very serious."' (p.117)

For all the differences in background, age and experience of life, Dad's fellow officers respected and liked him, and he them. In later years Dad used to speak warmly of a string of them, names which lodged themselves in my memory: Colonel 'Tug' Thornton, Colonel George Stobart, Colonel Grant Taylor, Colonel Orr, Colonel Forteath, Major Guy Stringer and Major Stacey, from many of whom cards used to arrive each Christmas in the 1950s.

There was the padre at Saugor, the Reverend Tony Lawrance whose wife Mary died in India. Dad used to tend her grave after Tony's return to England. Years later, when he remarried, Tony Lawrance wished Dad to be his best man, but it was not to be. For a while they had been out of touch with each other because of moving house. A little after the wedding, when they had re-established contact, the Lawrance's came to North Devon on holiday from their Rectory in Yorkshire – this was in 1952 – and Tony Lawrence gave us a puppy, 'Patch', from his English bull-terrier bitch.

Another of Dad's close friends was 'Nobby' Clark, who was also commissioned from among the warrant-officers at about the same time as Dad; Dad was godfather to his daughter, Georgina. To all of these men, Dad was known as 'Bill', as he had been throughout his Army life.

In July 1943, exactly three years after he was commissioned, Dad was promoted Captain; then, Acting Major in October 1943, and Temporary Major in January 1944 as the 'admin officer' at the Small Arms School. Sixty years later I met another Major who had served at Saugor.

He and his wife had lived in a bungalow only about fifty yards away from Dad and Mum in Haig Road. He told me that Dad was by then number two or three to Colonel Gray, the Commanding Officer at the school.

Everything was going well.

9
Matchmaking

IN JULY 1944, six months after he was promoted Major, Dad was visited at Saugor by Charlie Paul, his brother-in-law (Florrie's husband).

Charlie was a sergeant in the Royal Engineers. He was working in a railway operating company, as an instructor. His job was to teach men how to drive steam engines. Before the war he had still been a fireman, the driver's junior colleague on the footplate of steam engines, stoking up the fire to heat the boiler. In 1945 he had to return to that less-well-paid role on the Great Western Railway (GWR) until he gained afresh the promotion that he had won in the Sappers. The Army seems to have been more liberal than the demarcations and regulations imposed for decades by his union, the Association of Locomotive Engineers and Firemen (ASLEF), to which, as he fondly told me, he was devoted all his working life.

Charlie had come out from England via Ceylon (now Sri Lanka) and was travelling from Madras to Burma to join the campaign against Japan. He was granted permission to visit Dad on a short leave, and at 2pm on Monday, 24th July, Dad met Charlie at the height of the monsoon. It was raining as they met.

Q

It really was raining.

Until now I have been telling Dad's story from my memories of him, or from official or family documents, or from what Dad told Mum or me, and then, later, from the stories that Auntie Florrie passed on to me at our breakfasts and pasty dinners in Penzance.

But now I have on my desk Dad's diary and notebooks for 1944. He was forty-two years old. It was the year when the Allies closed in for

44

the kill on Germany, advancing relentlessly through Poland, Italy and France. It was the year when Dad was allowed to take his delayed home leave in England. It was the year when Dad met Mum and, only twelve days later, married her.

And this diary seems to me to be holy ground. It means so much to me not only because it is Dad's own personal record, in his hand, then still clear, elegant and firm. It is holy because it comes from the year that crowned all his successes.

It is holy for me, too, because of the way the story ended for Dad – and for his sisters, Clara and Kathleen; how it ended or will end or *may* end for all of us caught up in this dance, this *chorea* of St Vitus, from which there is no escape. But for a while, in 1944, all looked well for Dad and his sisters. For the moment no one in their family was affected by that horror, no one was ill. And I know that, whatever came later, when I understood it so poorly and made such mistakes, I am lucky that Dad *was* my father.

'Still raining,' Dad recorded that evening before going to bed. *'Had a good drink of beer and a bit of roast beef – what a chat we had about Home, too.'*

Charlie later wrote to Florrie and his children to tell them that Dad had arranged for him to be treated 'like royalty' during his time at Saugor.

And that was the evening when Uncle Charlie told Dad about Mum, and played the role of matchmaker. Short and stocky, with a dark Cornish complexion and thick black hair, down-to-earth, astute and full of common sense, Uncle Charlie was an unlikely candidate for this role.

Of course, Florrie must have taken the lead, for she and her sisters were concerned about their brother, who was surely lonely at times. One of his close colleagues and friends died that year, in middle age; and Dad's dog 'Tuppy', a Jack Russell terrier, also died. Dad's concern, too, for his fellow-officers' children is clear in the diary. He wished that Georgina, his goddaughter, could leave Saugor during the intense heat in the August of that summer, when he visited the grave of her stillborn brother at Pachmarhi. He was there on an inspection of the cantonment, the first time since 1939 that he had been able to visit his 'spiritual home' in the hills. He told Georgina's father, Nobby Clark, how much he wanted children of his own.

Perhaps it was the implausibility of Charlie's acting as a matchmaker, his solid reliability, which gave his words about Mum special force with Dad. About fifteen years later I occasionally met Uncle Charlie on the bus that I used to catch to school. He would be on his way to join a slightly unusual shift at the railway junction and marshalling yard to begin his day's work; it was not his regular bus. Uncle Charlie was always very kind to me. Perhaps there was something almost tender in his rugged look, well camouflaged by his engine driver's uniform and cap, smudged with Welsh coal, that said, 'But for my visit to Saugor in July 1944 to tell Jack about Grace, you would not be here.' And I recall how, on one of those mornings, he encouraged me to persevere in my studies, as he made his way past me along the gangway of the upper deck of the bus, with its notice enjoining 'No Spitting'.

On their second day together at Saugor Dad took Charlie for a walk around the ranges of the weapons school. They also went to see the farm and vegetable gardens that he managed. He kept sketches of the vegetable plots and lists of the names of the workers in his notebook.

Together, Dad and Charlie wrote letters Home to Florrie, Jack (Charlie's second son) and Kathleen, who was doing war-work at a factory in Gloucestershire which produced aircraft propellers. It was still raining as Dad and Charlie wrote. Already some 40 inches had fallen since the monsoon had started – *very good rains indeed*, Dad noted.

To round off the visit, Herbert and Jessie, friends with whom Dad sometimes stayed the night after the cinema show at the Club on Saturday evenings, visited Dad and met Charlie. They brought their

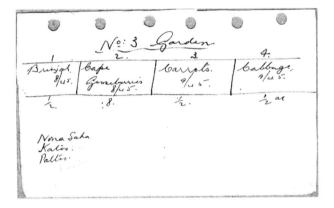

children with them. Then Charlie set off from Saugor to resume his journey to the frontier with Burma.

❦

What was it about Mum – Grace – as Charlie spoke about her that engaged Dad's interest? Her photographs from those years supply a ready answer, and surely Florrie had thoughtfully given Charlie some snaps to take to Saugor. Then, Grace had recently been freed from the responsibility of caring for her father and mother who had died in 1939 and 1943. She was still keeping house for her two bachelor brothers, Jack and George, rather against their inclination and certainly with little by way of thanks from them, but her mother's death the previous year left an enormous gap in her life that was aching to be filled.

But there was something else about her that I heard from a detached observer, who, in those years, watched Grace's family from a house across the road in Plympton and came to know them well after the War. She told me that she could tell that there was what she called 'something special' about Grace. She sensed an integrity and selfless loyalty. In part this showed itself in Mum's religious faith, which went beyond the rather routine Sunday observance of some in her family.

One way or another, Dad would have asked Charlie about this. From his diary you can see how much his faith mattered to him. Week by week he noted that he attended church on Sunday mornings and evenings, for matins and evensong. Often he also attended the early morning service of Holy Communion. Sometimes (for example on 4th June, Trinity Sunday that year), he records that he received the elements of the Communion, the bread wafer and the wine, although he had not yet been confirmed by a bishop.

The padre, Tony Lawrance, had done much to encourage Dad's faith. On 16th July, Dad records: *'Church 7pm. I read the lesson – the first time in my life.'* It was Tony Lawrance who offered Dad the privilege of receiving the Holy Communion before he was confirmed; this must have been very rare indeed in the Anglican Church in those days. Perhaps it was shyness about this that once prompted him to turn back when, on his way to St Peter's, he spotted that the commanding officer, Brigadier Cameron, was going there for the early service.

In September Tony Lawrance accompanied Dad to Jubbalpore where, on the sixth of the month, *'I was confirmed by the Bishop of Nagpur at 18.30 in the Garrison church.'*

Two years later this Bishop, Alec Hardie, stayed with Dad at his bungalow in Saugor. By then Mum had arrived in India, bringing me with her. Bishop Hardie allowed me to play a little with his hunter pocket watch, and commented to Mum that her son was a 'fine baby', so making a friend of her for life.

In the year that India became independent the Bishop wrote warmly of Dad as a person 'for whom I have the highest regard' and who had 'done more for the church in Saugor than any layman I have known there during the nine years in which I have been bishop of this diocese'. He refers to Dad as 'Church Secretary at Saugor'.

So when Charlie mentioned that Grace was confirmed and regularly went to Holy Communion, it surely rang a bell with Dad.

©

Forty-five years later Judy and I bought a cottage in East Sussex.

Mum was staying with us in London at the time of her birthday at the end of October. Judy was at work but I had a day off from the office, so Mum and I went to see the cottage a few weeks before we took possession of it. It was a golden autumn afternoon. The sun shone warmly in a slightly hazy blue sky. In the gardens the first bonfires of the season were giving out plumes of grey-white smoke from barrow-loads of fallen leaves.

We arrived at the cottage in the middle of the afternoon. It has a fine view along a wide valley in the Weald. Towards evening the sky over the valley often seems to reflect the light of the sea, fifteen miles away.

As Mum caught her first glimpse of the house, she said: *'It's a gentleman's residence'.* Then she added, *'Wouldn't Dad have loved it here? And keeping a few chickens...'?*

Her first comment was far from the truth, in the conventional sense. The cottage had been built for a farm labourer's family in 1932, although, as Thackeray* knew, there is no reason why a labourer should be any the less a gentleman than those who used to be accorded that

* 'Gentlemen ... Perhaps these are rarer personages than some of us think. Which of us can point to many such in his circle – men whose aims are generous, whose truth is constant, and not only constant in its kind but elevated in its degree; whose want of meanness makes them simple; who can look the world honestly in its face with an equal manly sympathy for the great and the small? We all know a hundred whose coats are well made, and a score who have excellent manners, and one or two happy beings who are what they call 'in the inner circle' and have shot into the very centre and bull's eye of the fashion; but of gentlemen, how many? Let each of us take a scrap of paper and each make out his list' – *Vanity Fair*, Part 2, Ch 62.

title in this world. But Mum's second comment was exactly right. Dad surely would have loved it here. Often, when I am working on the vegetable plot, I think of that.

The task of managing the smallholding that he showed to Charlie was more than just a job for Dad. The diagrams which he made carefully in 1945 to plan the crops to be grown that year, with the names of the Indian workers tending the separate parts of the holding, somehow show that. He kept them in his personal notebook. In his diary Dad also recorded, at various times, that he had had a rabbit hutch built; that some ducklings had hatched; that some cattle had arrived at Saugor. The farm was not a big part of his job, but he enjoyed it as an escape from the office.

A few years later, when I was three years old, we were living in a bungalow at St Ives in Cornwall. It is my second memory. Dad and I are together in our back garden: I am 'helping' him clean out the chicken house and their exercise pen. Wearing corduroy trousers, a jersey and his old trilby hat, Dad is stirring, in a *dixie* (Urdu for cooking pot), the mash with which he will feed the fowls.

'*Be careful, John, that's hot.*'

'*It isn't hot, Daddy, 'cos I eated a bit.*'

When one of our chickens died, or was somehow taken by a fox, he told me that it had flown away to Land's End, where I loved playing on the cliffs. All would be well at Land's End; all would be well.

He was such a gentle, tender-hearted, faithful, reliable, wise man. I am lucky that Uncle Charlie visited him at Saugor.

Soon after Dad had seen Charlie off from Saugor to rejoin his unit, he had to decide when to take the Home leave that had been delayed by the War.

10

Home Leave

ONE DAY at the end of July 1944 Dad recorded, *'Not feeling too well – a touch of tummy trouble in the evening.'* In fact, his medical notes show that the doctor diagnosed that he was suffering from mild dysentery. A few days later he received a letter from Charlie, by then diverted to Julandar, now Jullundur, in the Punjab, where, at Amritsar, he visited the Sikhs' Golden Temple.

The Allies' victories and advance in Europe now made it possible for Dad to be released for Home leave. It would mean an absence from Saugor of three and a half months in all. Dad noted that there was *'a chance to go Home – but, I'll wait until the summer* [of 1945].'

He was longing to see England again. The previous October he had copied out Shakespeare's words on a sheet of writing paper to keep beside him (King *Richard the Second*, II, i, 42ff).

While the offer of Home leave was still on the table, Dad visited Pachmarhi and inspected the station where he had worked so happily for ten years. Then, on his return to Saugor at the end of August, he wrote in his diary: *'Sent in my name for leave in September!'*

51

Perhaps it was Charlie's letter, jogging his memory about what they had discussed during his visit to Saugor, that caused Dad to change his mind. Perhaps it was the visit to Pachmarhi, with its more temperate climate, and then the sudden return to the intense heat at Saugor that made a visit Home seem more attractive. Perhaps confidence in the Allies' steady progress in Europe played its part. Perhaps the plans for his confirmation the following month gave him hope and encouraged him to think that it was now the time to go. Whatever it was that prompted him, he was resolving his future.

Dad began to *'prepare his boxes'* for home. He wrote to his sister Clara at Madron near Penzance and told her that he was coming. On 2nd September, the eve of the fifth anniversary of the British declaration of war on Germany, he recorded: *'The news from Home is marvellous. Our troops crossed the Belgian border at 11.00 hours today.'* The next day was declared by the King to be a Day of Thanksgiving, and, at St Peter's church, *'there was a good congregation. Guy* [Stringer, an old friend] *took the collection with me.'* Dad's confirmation at Jubbalpore took place three days later.

On 16th September Dad received the details of his travel home *'via Deolali'*, and he was *'very busy packing up'*. He left Saugor on the eighteenth, and sailed from Bombay on the twenty-seventh. The journey by way of the Suez Canal, which took twenty-seven days, amounted to some 6,260 miles, according to his atlas, in which he had been marking the Allies' progress in Europe since D-Day. He arrived in England, probably at Liverpool, on 24th October. He travelled by train to Devonshire and stayed with Florrie in Plympton for a few days before moving on to Penzance.

℺

At the end of her life, lying in her bed in hospital but with her mind and memory still clear and reliable, Mum told me of her first glimpse of Dad. She was working upstairs at home, making the beds for Jack and George.

> *'I looked out of the bedroom window, and there he was, walking along with Florrie's children, so handsome and tall, and he looked so nice.'*

It was 28th October, a Saturday. After walking from Florrie and Charlie's house along Stone Barton to Plympton station, the route which gave Mum the chance to catch that sight of them, Dad *'went up to*

Dartmoor with Jack, Doris and Coulson'. They travelled on the branch-line of the railway via Marsh Mills, up the valley of the River Plym to Yelverton and then across the open moor to Princetown. At 1,400 feet this was the highest railway station in England, serving the little town and the prison built in the Napoleonic Wars.

On Sunday Dad attended a service at St Mary's church with Terry, Florrie's eldest son. Mum was probably in the congregation at that service. It was her thirty-fifth birthday.

℘

The next morning Dad caught the 8.40 train to Penzance. He went to Madron to stay with Clara and her husband Charlie Semmens. He wrote and underlined:

'Very nice to be Home again.'

Kathleen arrived on leave from her war-work, *'looking very well'*.

On Wednesday Dad *'went over to Newlyn to see them all'*. On Thursday he visited *'town* [Penzance] *with Clara and Charlie'*, and took Kathleen to a meal at the Ritz Hotel there. At around this date the set lunch at an excellent hotel in the West of England cost four shillings (20p):

Vegetable soup
Fried fillet of plaice with anchovy sauce
Roast lamb or Cold Buffet
Apple tart – thick cream
Cheese and biscuits
Dessert

On Saturday Dad *'went to Newlyn for the fish'*. He loved fresh fish, just caught in the sea on which his family had worked for generations. How he must have longed for it in India. On Sunday he attended St Peter's church, Newlyn, at 11am and 6pm, just as he and his sisters had done for so long as children.

The weather was changeable, but one day Dad went for a walk to Morvah, Pendeen (where Florrie had been in service twenty years earlier), St Just and Land's End. It was a march of at least twenty miles. He arrived home by 6pm after a late start because it had been raining in the morning. He was very fit. Next, he spent a day with Nora and her husband Reg.

The routine of family events continued until the middle of the month, with teas together, church, and a visit to the cinema to see *For Whom The Bell Tolls*. On his last day with the family he enjoyed another long walk, from Penzance to Sancreed and back *'by 14.15 hours'*.

On the day after that walk Dad went by train to Southampton to stay with his old friends, John and Emma, who had retired to England from India a little while earlier. It took nine hours to reach Southampton from Penzance, and the weather was *'very cold'* throughout Dad's two days there. John introduced him to his sister – perhaps in an attempt at matchmaking. Kathleen, too, had sent him a photograph of herself and two friends with whom she worked in the factory; *'the three glamour girls'*, she wrote on the back.

On 18th November Dad made another nine-hour journey, to his sister Rene and her husband Harold in Bushbury, a couple of miles north of Wolverhampton. Rene met him at the station. *'All looking well,'* he wrote. Their daughter, Megan, fourteen years old at the time, recalls Dad arriving in his uniform at their house in Kipling Road. She remembers his 'lovely dark grey eyes' and sunburnt complexion and moustache. Her brother Graham, then eleven years old, remembers him as a 'lovely, kind uncle', with an upright, military bearing. Dad was interested in the linnet and greenfinch that Rene kept, and every evening he carefully covered the birdcage to enable them to roost peacefully and have a good sleep. He used to do just the same for our two successive canaries, each of them called Chippy, in the 1950s.

While he was staying with Rene, Dad went to Stone in Staffordshire for a day: *'a grand day with Guy Stringers' people. Home by 9pm.'* He visited Harold's family, the Corfields, and 'Maria' for tea; Rene was probably matchmaking this time. He took Rene to the cinema to see *'Dr. Wassal'* – *'bed 00.45'* – on Friday, and a play, *Nothing But The Truth*, on Saturday.

On both his Sundays at Rene's he went to church. On the first, Rene came to meet him after the service – he wrote in his diary that in the service they had sung *Jesus Shall Reign*, a favourite hymn of his. On the second Sunday he went to the local church in Bushbury in the morning and to St Peter's, the parish church of Wolverhampton, in the evening. By the second Sunday, 26th November, he was again finding the weather *'very cold'*.

On Monday morning Dad left for Plymouth. The journey took twelve and a half hours. At North Road station, his nephew Jack met him and took him back to Florrie and Charlie's. Kathleen was also staying there for a couple of days. Dad took her to Plymouth to have a portrait photograph taken. It is a beautiful picture, which, as it turned out, caught her calm grace and gentle features just in time. Within a year or two her mind and body, and with them the peace you can sense in her expression in that photograph, would begin to be destroyed by Huntington's.

In Plympton there were more family outings. Dad went on a walk with his nephew Jack through Plymbridge woods to Roborough, a village on the edge of Dartmoor.

He took Florrie, her daughter Doris, and Florrie's best friend, Hilda (Mum's elder sister), to see *The White Cliffs of Dover* at the cinema. This popular film was based on the verses of the American poet Alice Duer Miller. She had died in 1942, having caught in her poetry, from the point of an 'outsider', as she depicted her heroine, something of what enabled her adopted country to survive those years and, finally, achieve victory:

> *I have loved England, dearly and deeply,*
> *Since the first morning, shining and pure ...*
> *When they pointed the white cliffs of Dover,*
> *Startled, I found there were tears on my cheek ...*
>
> *The tree of liberty grew and changed and spread,*
> *But the seed was English ...*
> *In a world where England is finished and dead,*
> *I do not wish to live.*

On Sunday, Dad travelled to Totnes to visit a friend, Frank, and stayed the night. He went to church there on Sunday morning and arrived *'Home again by 3pm'*.

On Monday, 4th December, Dad and Mum met for the first time. They walked together to Lee Moor, a village on the southern fringe of Dartmoor.

It was the start of a twelve-day courtship.

11
Mum

MUM'S FAMILY was poor; nothing like as hard-pressed as Dad and his sisters during their childhood and youth, but poor nevertheless. She told me that when she was helping her mother keep house in the 1920s and 1930s and they were dusting and sweeping together, she used to take up a piece of coconut matting in the little back drawing-room in order to clean the floor. There was no carpet in the family home, no. 7, Stone Barton, in those days. There never was, except for special occasions when they borrowed one. Many families lived like that.

Mum loved school and worked hard at her lessons. She became head girl. She did well enough in her studies for Mr Baple, the headmaster, to encourage her parents to put her in for the scholarship examination for the grammar school. Sir Joshua Reynolds, the portrait painter and first President of the Royal Academy, and far and away Plympton's most distinguished son, had been educated there.

Nothing came of Mr Baple's idea because there was not enough money to buy the uniform and text books she would have needed at the grammar school. Mum would have done well there, but she never gave the slightest hint of resentment at her loss. Even with most of her older brothers and sisters already at work and making some contribution to the family's income, she could see that funds were short.

Her brother Walter, three years older than Mum and the youngest of the five brothers in the family, had passed the scholarship and gone to Plymouth Corporation Grammar School. He was the first and last of that generation to enjoy this advantage. Mum was proud of his success.

She cried when, near the end of her life, she told me that on one occasion some pupils at the grammar school jeered at him because of the patches and darns in his school uniform, lovingly and carefully mended by their mother.

Both of Mum's parents, Henry and Agnes, had been in domestic service. It was a family tradition.

In 1895, at the age of twenty-eight, they married in London. With Mum's arrival fourteen years later, they completed their family of eight children – five sons and three daughters. During those years they were often on the move around England, in service with various families, first in Yorkshire, and later in Worcestershire and the West of England.

After working at Tehiddy House in Cornwall, where Mum was born, the family moved to Plymouth. For two years Henry and Agnes kept a sweetshop there. It was unprofitable. According to Mum, her parents were overgenerous to many of the local children as well as their own. Perhaps it was as a toddler, in the sweetshop, that she gained her life-long taste for liquorice and chocolate.

In 1912 the family moved to Plympton St Mary, five miles east of Plymouth. Henry became butler to the Strode family at Newnham House. The ten of them lived in a three-bedroom terraced house at no. 12, Moorland View. Ten years later the family moved to no. 7, Stone Barton, one of the houses being built on a small new council estate on the other side of the village. To celebrate their move and to mark her thirteenth birthday, Mum planted a lilac tree beside the front door.

At about the same time Henry suffered a serious heart attack, and he had to retire. Dr Stamp told Agnes that her husband had not many months to live. His heart trouble often made his sallow, square face and his bald head flush, and become red. Agnes was determined to keep Henry alive and well. *'She treated him like gold dust'*, and gave him a healthy diet with no red meat, fat or cream, Mum told me.

The family used to gather to sing around the piano in the drawing-room where Mum played for them. They were proud of their piano, engraved in gilt letters, *'W. Daneman and Company, London, 1883'*. When Henry was butler at Tehiddy House, their sons had loaded it on to a donkey cart at William Chandler's 'Piano and Music Salon' in Redruth and brought it the three or four miles to their tied cottage. In those days

Agnes had also played the piano, and in due course she bequeathed it to Mum.

Agnes was a beloved matriarch, in charge of the day-to-day running of the house. She, rather than Henry, had the brains in their long and successful partnership.

'She was endowed with a great capacity for loving people. She was marvellous: she gave everything to them,' my cousin John told me. *'She and grandfather generated a very happy, lively atmosphere, with never any strain except for his turns of ill health.'*

Ⓠ

Dad never met Mum's parents.

Henry died in late October 1939. His death, Agnes realised, was hastened by the despair and anxiety that he felt because of the second German war in his lifetime. She shared that feeling, but his damaged heart soon gave in to the strain.

Mum had greeted Henry at the front door, as usual, on his return from his daily 'constitutional'. She had already cut the bread and spread it with margarine for his tea. The kettle was bubbling on the range. The teapot was warming. As Mum took her father's Homburg hat and walking stick from him, he fell dead in her arms. It was the eve of her thirtieth birthday.

Agnes lived on for nearly four years.

One night in July 1943 during the blitz of Plymouth, she decided to sit outside in the garden and watch the flames rising high into the sky from the horrifying fires as the bombs fell on the city. The heat in the stuffy shelter had made her feel unwell, and she did not want to stay there for the whole of the alert. Well into the night she was hit by the blast from a bomb dropped by a German bomber as it sped eastwards, making its getaway from the anti-aircraft defences that surrounded Plymouth.

Agnes took to her bed and died a few days later, surrounded by her children.

Mum went wild with grief. For more than ten years she had been caring for elderly parents and two curmudgeonly brothers, with little joy, help or encouragement.

Her life had begun to grow darker after the distressing death, five years earlier, of her brother Arthur, caused by the re-infection with tuberculosis of a wound to his back that he had suffered as a boy. The loss of her dearest brother, coming so early in his promising life, was to haunt Mum for the rest of her days. He was only thirty-four at the time of his death.

Arthur's death, those of her parents, the unending pressure of the war and the thankless drudgery of looking after Jack and George, knocked Mum off balance. The prospects looked bleak. She was thirty-three years old and most of the eligible men were married or away in the Services at the War. She had never lacked admirers, and she soon found herself briefly engaged to Les.

One afternoon early in August, Grace gave way to her grief for her mother. She mixed together half a bottle of gin and brandy in a strong cocktail, and began to play the piano. She very rarely drank alcohol, and the effect was extreme. In the little back drawing-room, she told me, the piano began to sway to and fro under the powerful attack of her normally lyrical, sensitive fingers. Various members of the family gathered in the little hallway and peered around the door from time to time. Finally, someone led her upstairs to recover in her bedroom, at the front of the house. From her window she caught sight of Les and called out to him, *'Go to hell, you bugger!'*

Mum was no fool. For all her simplicity of soul and singleness of heart, she did not miss much. People underestimated her intelligence, or her insight into the devices and desires of those around her, at their peril.

As it turned out, the word that Mum used was apt but completely uncharacteristic of her. Les was later discovered to be the boy-friend of her cousin George, a married man who lived with his family in Nottingham. The two of them, Les and George, were thereafter always known as 'Lamb' and 'Lettuce'.

The next day, chastened and overwhelmed by guilt, Grace returned the engagement ring to Les, who primly told her to wash her mouth out with disinfectant and to go to church to pray for forgiveness. Without a doubt, she did the latter. She 'signed the pledge' and on that day became teetotal. Apart from the brandy on the plum pudding at Christmas, and in her last years an occasional spoonful of it when she felt, in her word, *'squawmish'*, she kept her pledge.

That action was not enough, on its own, to restore Mum's equilibrium.

She was courted by Charles Smith, a naval officer, who gave her an unofficial engagement ring. He also gave her some romantic piano music

– Liszt's *Liebestraum no. 3* and *A maiden's prayer* by T. Badarzewska. Mum wrote on them 'From Chas to Grace'.*

It was around this time in 1944, not long after the humiliating nadir of Grace's fortunes, that Charlie Paul visited Dad at Saugor and spoke to him of her. Everyone in their families must have seen what both Jack and Grace needed.

And, despite her reaction to the loss of her mother, Charlie had good reason to be confident of what he told Dad about Mum. As the shrewd witness who lived across the road from no.7, Stone Barton told me after Mum's death, *'I could see that there was something special about her. It was her integrity.'*

---

* 'Chas' did not prove to be the answer to her prayer. After a long gap caused by his service at sea, he appeared one day on the doorstep at No.7. He discovered that Grace had married and taken her infant son to India. When her brother Jack opened the door and gave him the news, Charles Smith said, 'I would have married her.' Jack, always laconic, replied, 'Well, you're too late.'

12

Courtship and Marriage

FIFTY YEARS LATER, in the early 1990s, Mum's independent days at home were drawing to an end. She had been a widow for twenty years, and she was determined to stay on as long as possible in the house where she and Dad had made their final home. They had lived there for most of their twenty seven and a half years together.

We did whatever practical things we could to help her, but it was more important, generally, to try to keep up her spirits and encourage her. One thing I did was to suggest that, on the long winter evenings when time hung heavy for her, she should write an account of some of her happy memories: *'things that made us happy years ago,'* I said. Mum took to the idea, a little reluctantly at first, and it used to improve her spirits.

As she sat by the coal fire in the sitting-room in the evening, or at the kitchen table in the morning with her back to the comforting warmth of the Rayburn, converted from anthracite to oil soon after Dad's death, she put down on paper some of her thoughts and memories. She relived her happy days, and wrote them up in an old Basildon Bond writing pad, of the sort so endearingly used by Sir Alec Douglas Home to draft his speeches when, briefly, he was Prime Minister in 1963 – 1964.

One day she wrote:

'December 4th 1994 ... this is 50 years to the day since I first met Jack ... Next day we went by train from Plympton station to Totnes and then to Buck-fastleigh. It was wonderful. We had a meal at the British Restaurant, of

casserole and Manchester pudding. Then to a pub in Totnes where I treated him to a glass of beer. He was a really kind *gentleman, and I think that we knew that we would marry.'*

At Buckfast Abbey a French monk was playing the violin, and the sound filled the peaceful building. There was no one else there.

In his pocket diary Dad kept a brief record of the events of those twelve busy days:

'Tuesday 5th. Took Grace to Buckfast Abbey and Totnes. A lovely day.

Wednesday 6th. Took Grace to Shaugh [in the Plym valley]. *Whitethorn* [the pub where they had lunch]. *Bed 2am.*

Thursday 7th. Went to Heybrook Bay with Grace – a lovely day.

Friday 8th. Afternoon went to Meavy Church, Clearbrook with Grace. Skylark Inn.

Saturday 9th. Saw Chaplain! [to arrange their wedding] *We went up to fix up rooms at Two Bridges but no luck. Arranged at* Dartmeet.

Sunday 10th. Church with Hilda and Wally am. Meavy with Grace pm. Bed 2.30am.

Monday 11th. Left for Nora's. Very nice trip down.

Tuesday 12th. Up to Clara's; and packed a box.

Wednesday 13th. Left 9.30. Met Grace at North Road station. Lunch and then to Shaugh and Dewerstone.

Thursday 14th. Went to buy the rings at Page's in Plymouth but only took one. Had tea at Goodbody's. Did a lot of other shopping with Grace.

Friday 15th. Went with Grace and bought the engagement ring. Tea at Goodbody's, then to Plymbridge and walk home.

Saturday 16th. Married at 2pm in Plympton Church. We had a very nice party after the wedding. Left at 4.30pm for Dartmeet – Mrs. James – a very quiet and beautiful house, and the country is thrilling.'

And in her pale blue Basildon Bond pad Mum wrote:

'December 16th 1994. This would be Dad's and my Golden Wedding. Fifty years ago at Stone Barton we prepared for our wedding at St. Mary's church. They carried up the carpet from Wal and Audrey's house on Plymouth Road, the stair carpet from Hilda and Fred's house [a little further along Stone Barton at no. 84, on the other side of the road], *and made no. 7 look very smart.*

The table was spread in the back room, and a great spread it was, although rationing was still on. Hilda got black-market food via Tom the policeman. The church was quite full. Jack [her brother] *gave me away; Dad was very smart in his officer's uniform and me in a blue dress – very plain, but a buttonhole of red roses. The room was cram-full of family and neighbours. I played the piano, and John* [Hilda's son] *and Terry* [Florrie's eldest son] *sang and the rest of us joined in. Mr. Scott – our next-door neighbour – said that it was the best wedding he had ever attended.*

The taxi came, driven by Joan Littlejohns. The family and friends all made a long line on each side of the path to the gate. Jack and I went to get in the taxi, bound for Dartmeet, to the strains of 'I'll Be with You in Apple Blossom Time'. It was pelting with rain.

The next day it was just like summer and we went for a lovely walk on Dartmoor. Stayed there for two weeks. Then had a week in London! We went to several shows. Called to see Uncle Jack and Aunt Nellie at their flat.

It was sad when Jack's last day came, and he left the hotel to board the ship to travel back to India; me to return to Plympton.'

On the last day of 1944 Mum wrote a message for Dad in his diary:

'We're at the Zoo – very nice. At the present moment we're contemplating roast beef very eagerly – frosty day and we're a trifle peckish. Been to Uncle Jack's yesterday and had a lovely supper. They like Jack, I can see. No wonder. He's such a dear.

Now we've had hot bath and are ready for bed. It's New Year's Eve and London is like a mad place. Our last night together.

After tomorrow is gone, may time fly until I see my lovely husband again. The world will be a very empty place when he's away from me. We are married, tho', and have the lovely future to look forward to.

May God bless him and keep him safe until we meet again.'

As Dad embraced Mum before leaving her, he quoted Shakespeare:

> *'Parting is such sweet sorrow*
> *That I shall say goodnight till it be morrow.'*

But Mum was not entirely alone as she returned to Plympton.

PART TWO

13

'One hundred and five, North Tower'

CHROMOSOME 4, gene IT15, a few specks of matter.

Sometimes, perhaps in sixty cases in a million, a fault is there. No one knows why. It just happens. The coding of the gene is extended a little, and that unnecessary extension is the cause of it all.

If the fault is there in the gene, it leads to Huntington's chorea, Huntington's disease, usually in middle age. And a child of someone with the disease has a 50-50 chance of inheriting the faulty gene; it never skips a generation.

It is as simple as that: a 50-50 chance, the toss of a coin.

But perhaps something more powerful than fate is at work here.

In *A Tale of Two Cities*, the only words that Dr Alexandre Manette could say when he was freed from the Bastille were 'One hundred and five, North Tower'. For a while, until his daughter Lucy's care and tenderness had healed him, that amounted to Dr Manette's whole identity.

Dad was so much more than Chromosome 4, gene IT15 *'extended'*.

Throughout the twenty-eight years after his marriage he poured himself out for us. He emptied himself and spent himself and everything that he had in order to care for us. He set us safely on our way.

His care for us lasted until his final days.

'Are you all right for money, Grace?' he used to ask Mum in hospital, when his voice was almost gone.

In some way, to the tiny extent then possible, Dad remained master of his fate.

14

Home Thoughts from Abroad

AFTER DAD had set off at the beginning of January 1945 on his return to India for the last time, Mum returned to Devonshire secretly carrying me within her.

Just after Germany's unconditional surrender to the Allies on 7th May, Charlie Paul wrote a letter to Dad. Charlie's unit was working to move troops and supplies eastwards into Burma in order to halt and reverse the Japanese invasion.

Charlie told Dad that he had heard from Florrie that Mum was finding it difficult now to summon up much enthusiasm for the thankless task of cooking and cleaning and caring for her brothers, Jack and George. Dad underlined some sentences in Charlie's letter and put an exclamation mark in the margin, drawn in the thick, Army-issue red pencil of the sort I remember, red at one end and blue at the other. As little boys we used to practise writing and drawing with a few that had survived.

Apart from keeping house for Jack and George, Mum spent some weeks early in 1945 helping Wally and her sister-in-law Audrey, who had recently given birth to her second son. She loved Audrey and recalled it as a great comedy that once, when Audrey was reclining in bed with her infant son she called out to her, as she was doing the housework downstairs, *'You may take the cream now, Grace.'*

Mum also found herself nursing back to health her Canadian cousin Ted, who had been a prisoner of war in Germany. Ted was the grandson of her mother's sister, who had emigrated from England to Canada after the First World War.

In 1940 Ted had bravely volunteered to come to England for service in the Royal Canadian Air Force at a time when Canadians in their armed forces had the right to choose to serve only in North America. Two years later, flying on a joint RAF/RCAF mission, he was shot down over France. Betrayed to the Germans by the French peasants who found him, he was taken to a prison camp in Germany, far to the east. He was held in the part of Germany that was given to Poland after the War when that country's eastern and western borders were moved two hundred miles to the west.

By 1945 Ted was emaciated. He was forced by his German guards to march west as they fled with their prisoners to escape the merciless horrors of the revenge exacted by the advancing Soviet Army. After his release by the British and a stay at the hospital for Canadian servicemen at Cliveden, he moved down to Devon to live for a while with Mum in Plympton. He was still only skin and bone, and the sight of him preyed on the mind of Florrie's fifteen-year-old son Jack.

Ted depended almost exclusively on Mum for his care during that time when he was recovering from what, as he later recalled, was an almost deranged state. He then went back to Canada and soon married Mary. Only in 1997 as he came to the last years of his life, could he bring himself to revisit France. From the safety of the Eurostar train he gazed on the fields where he had hidden his parachute in 1942 and been betrayed by the peasants whom he had taken for friends.

Mum did not have an easy pregnancy. She had no one to care for her at no. 7 during the three months after my birth; rather, she had to care for me in addition to her brothers. She had to work very hard, and developed varicose veins.

She endured a difficult, listless year.

Throughout that year Dad wrote to her almost every day. When she set off for India to join him in January 1946, she left all these letters at no. 7, safe in a box lined with pink satin, bequeathed to her by her mother. She had carefully tied them together in bundles with ribbons. On her return to England in the autumn of 1947, Mum was horrified to find that Jack and George had sold the inlaid box, and had thrown out Dad's letters and the other small treasures that her mother had left her in her informal will, together with £8 in cash.

None of Dad's letters survives, but he used to copy out lines of poetry to send to Mum to soothe, comfort and encourage her. In his copy of Palgrave's *Golden Treasury* he annotated the verses that he sent her, with her name and the date when he wrote. This little blue volume, in the *Oxford World Classics* series, became precious to her, and in later years she often turned to it as a secure reminder of what she and Dad shared at that time, memories of their happiness.

After so long in India, twenty-three years by then, Dad's thoughts were becoming focused on settling down in England and the sort of home he and Mum might make. As the greatest heat of summer built up in the centre of the subcontinent, just before Midsummer Day, he copied out and sent to Mum some lines by Samuel Rogers (1763-1855):

A WISH

Mine be a cot beside the hill;
   A bee-hive's hum shall soothe my ear;
A willowy brook that turns a mill,
   With many a fall shall linger near.

The swallow, oft, beneath my thatch
   Shall twitter from her clay-built nest;
Oft shall the pilgrim lift the latch,
   And share my meal, a welcome guest.

Around my ivied porch shall spring
   Each fragrant flower that drinks the dew;
And Lucy, at her wheel, shall sing
   In russet gown and apron blue.

The village church among the trees,
   Where first our marriage vows were given,
With merry peels shall swell the breeze
   And point with taper spire to Heaven.

The 'cottage beside a hill' would become real within three years. A few days later he sent Mum these lines by Robert Browning:

HOME THOUGHTS FROM ABROAD

Oh, to be in England now that April's there,
And whoever wakes in England sees, some morning, unaware,
That the lowest boughs and the brushwood sheaf
Round the elm tree bole are in tiny leaf,
While the chaffinch sings on the orchard bough
In England – now!

The last lines of the second stanza of these 'Home Thoughts' express how strongly Home must have been calling Dad:

> *And though the fields look rough with hoary dew,*
> *All will be gay when noontide wakes anew*
> *The buttercups, the little children's dower*
> *– Far brighter than this gaudy melon flower!*

For all his longing to go Home and settle down, Dad and his colleagues in India had a pressing sense of the size and urgency of what they had to do before they could relax. In his copy of the anthology *England*, compiled in 1944 by Harold Nicolson, Dad marked some lines in Rudyard Kipling's poem 'For All We Have and Are', written in 1914:

> *There is but one task for all –*
> *One life for each to give.*
> *What stands if Freedom fall?*
> *Who dies if England live?*

Many years after Dad's death, in the Family Bible that he had bought in May 1934, I found a sheet of paper to which he had pasted some flowers and leaves sent to him by Mum, with the following notes made by him:

> *Wallflower*
> *Bluebell from Plymbridge*
> *Beech leaf*
> *Briar rose from Plymbridge.*
>
> 3rd June 1945

Dad was full of hope. He had a strong faith that God ordered this world to our good, if only we cooperate with Him in His way. In July he sent Mum more lines by Browning. They came from *Pippa Passes*, the song that the innocent girl sang for the joy of life, despite her hardships and ragged clothes:

> *The year's at the spring,*
> *And day's at the morn;*
> *Morning's at seven;*
> *The hillside's dew-pearled;*

The lark's on the wing;
The snail's on the thorn;
God's in his heaven –
All's right with the world!

Dad wrote some of his letters to Mum from Saugor on the verandah of his graceful, airy, detached bungalow, surrounded by a garden with flowers and trees. A watercolour of the bungalow and garden was painted for him by his friend, Major Hicks, at the end of September. It shows the shrubs and the elegant mohwa trees with their plum-coloured flowers (Plate 10).

This Indian Army bungalow was far and away the most comfortable house he had ever lived in, and it was the place where his own family life would begin. The bungalow still stands in Haig Road, now shared by two Indian Army officers.

The picture reveals another aspect of Dad's hopes. On the right is drawn the sturdy, wooden frame of a swing that he had put there in preparation for his first child's arrival.

And, a week after the watercolour was painted, I was born in circumstances far safer and more luxurious than anything ever enjoyed by any member of my parents' families in any generation. I was lucky to arrive in Whincroft nursing home, Horrabridge, near Buckland Monarchorum on the edge of Dartmoor.

The stress of separation from Dad, of caring for her brothers and sister-in-law, and of nursing Ted was telling on Mum. The doctor attending her called her 'the excitable lady from Plympton'.

A month after my birth Mum received her first and only passport, number 11274, dated 5th November. It records her details:

height – 5'10';
colour of eyes – brown;
colour of hair – brown;
special peculiarities, ——;
British Subject by birth;
wife of British Subject;
one child;
countries for which this passport is valid – British Empire.

The adventure in India was to be Mum's only travel abroad. She must have been nervous. Her old friend Vi Luxon, a regular worshipper with

her at the early 8am Holy Communion at St Mary's, gave her a beauti-
fully illuminated card, kept for ever in the Family Bible:

> ... *Renew our faith that we may feel Thee near*
> *Lest we forget Thee in our childish fear;*
> *Amid the turmoil let us know Thy Will*
> *And hear Thy tender whisper,* Peace, be still.

At the beginning of January Dad was appointed MBE (Military
Division) in the New Year's honours list. Brigadier Cameron, his commanding officer, wrote to him that it was *'for a job well done'*.

On 10th January 1946 Mum took a taxi from no. 7 Stone Barton.
She collected her sister Hilda at no. 84, and then her brother Wally
at his house on Plymouth Road. The two of them came with us on the
train from North Road station in Plymouth to see us off at Liverpool
docks.

On the twelfth, Mum embarked for India. She had to share a cabin
with a mother and her twelve-year-old daughter, both of them selfish
and unhelpful. Mum was afraid whenever she had to leave me on my
own with them for a few minutes. They stole a brooch that Dad had
given her. We disembarked at Bombay (now also called Mumbai) on 1st
February.

Fifty years later Mum wrote:

> *'I left Stone Barton for India ... the family coming to Liverpool on the train –*
> *first class. Leaving them to go on the ship – the Drottningholm, a Swedish*
> *vessel. A month's travelling – arriving at Bombay and meeting Jack, with John*
> *in the pram, and staying with friends of Jack's – then travelling to Saugor*
> *after riding around Bombay in a tonga. Train to Saugor – arriving at bunga-*
> *low and saying, 'Will I have to whitewash the ceiling?' (a joke!) – a huge room.*
> *Happy times at Saugor – lovely garden, birds and flowers. John growing all*
> *the time ... then leaving to come home when John was two.'*

Mother also wrote, on another occasion:

> *'I've just remembered our lovely bungalow in India. The garden was filled*
> *with flowerbeds and a great many tubs of roses, and a lovely birdbath in which*
> *parakeets of every colour bathed, and golden oriole and hoopoe. The mali*

(gardener) used to keep the flowers well watered. We had two bearers – Kalloo and Kundan – and a cook. A little boy used to pull the punkah (fan) to keep air flowing through.

We went for walks early morning and late evening. The trees were lovely, covered in flowers. On one morning walk we saw a cobra, and Margo, our lovely white bull terrier, chased it. Dad threw a stone at it and it slid down a hole; apparently the insects irritated it and it came up to get cool and the eagles took it ... We also had a beautiful white pony named Joey ...

Another night Dad went to kneel down beside our bed to say his prayers and he noticed a giant poisonous scorpion there, just in time. He took his shoe and managed to kill it.'

Life was full of the kind of dangers unknown to a country girl from Devonshire:

'The robbers came one night and stole our canteen of silver cutlery and lots more of our wedding presents. Margo barked, but she was locked in; maybe we would not have lost our things if she had been free.

One day we had a picnic in the jungle with Jim Byam Shaw and Margaret, his wife ...'

In his account of his early life, entitled *George*, Emlyn Williams mentions Jim Byam Shaw, brother of Glen, a leading director and producer with whom Williams later worked in London when he achieved great success as a playwright. Williams met Jim Byam Shaw at Oxford in the Michaelmas term of 1923. That term Williams, from North Wales, and A.L. Rowse, from Cornwall, went up as scholars to Christ Church. To win a scholarship at such a grand college was an astounding achievement. Each of them came from a home correctly reckoned to be very poor, although their autobiographies make it clear that their parents were, in fact, much better off than Dad's family.

Emlyn Williams wrote: 'I made friends. The first was a tall diffident youth named Byam Shaw, who noticed that I was reading the theatre page and told me he had a young brother, Glen, who was on tour playing the boy in At Mrs. Beam's.'

Perhaps Jim noticed that, like the young Emlyn Williams, Mum needed to be reassured that she fitted in. He went on to become a distinguished art historian and returned, in later life, to Christ Church to catalogue their collection of art. But Mum's recollection of him was as Dad's friend, a kindly man, middle-aged (he was forty-three years old in 1946) but youthful in manner, who, for all his scholarship, even in the heat of India, loved to polish his own shoes.

Jim was a good friend to both of them, as was Margaret, who died a year or so later. For years, in the 1950s, Jim used to send Dad and Mum a magnificent Christmas card from the Athenaeum in London. Their kindness to Mum was important to her. Adrian Rouse, an officer twenty years younger than Jim who became Dad's friend when he attended a course at Saugor, remembered Mum as an anxious, country girl.

Mum found it difficult to adapt to an alien life. Audrey, who a few months earlier had called to Mum with the invitation to take the cream downstairs, was later disappointed that India had not made her more sophisticated: it was, she told Mum, just as if she had gone down to the shop in the neighbouring village of Colebrook for some groceries.

The truth was that Mum could not change like a chameleon to match her circumstances. This immutability, in her case, was so bound up with her integrity and resolution that it saved us all in the long run; we would have sunk without it after Dad's ill health became critical, and then in the years after his death. But it must have made life difficult in smaller things, especially in India. Kindness such as that of Jim and Margaret helped her. It also helped Dad, who was more able than anyone to appreciate and enjoy Mum's ingenuous enthusiasm and eccentricity. His detached, wry good humour helped her not to take life too seriously, which was perhaps her way.

There were others, a good number of them, whom Mum recalled with gratitude and affection. Colonel 'Tug' Thornton, who used to soak up his gravy at dinner with a piece of bread; Joan Forteath, wife of another colonel, for whom she made Cornish pasties; Molly Stacey, wife of a major, who said to her, *'Go on, Grace, pick him up,'* when I was crying in my cot. All of them helped her to cope. There was her delight in nature, her interest in the flowers, birds and animals, and, in fact, in all the different races and religions represented in the Army, like the bearded Sikhs and the tall, proud Pathans whom she caught sight of when she took me in the pram on the road around the practice ranges at the Small Arms School.

Then there was her music, the officers' ball, and the parties held at various bungalows. Mum was a gifted pianist and used to accompany others. Once, at a party, she suggested to the officer she was playing for that they perform the sentimental ballad 'Trees'. *'Spare me that, Mrs.*

Symons, spare me that,' he replied, and his dry response raised Mum's
spirits whenever she thought of it, even on her deathbed.

Many pieces of sheet music, stamped 'Rose and Company, Fort,
Bombay (telegrams *"Rosebud Bombay"*)', made their way to her in those
days at Saugor: the 'Destiny Waltz' by Sydney Baynes (2 rupees), 'Bells
Across the Meadow' by Albert Ketelbey (2 rupees, 8 annas), 'Nights of
Gladness' by Charles Ancliffe (2 rupees).

There was St Peter's church. Dad and Mum used to take it in turns
to attend the Holy Communion service at eight o'clock on Sunday
mornings, leaving the other to stay in the bungalow with me. By this
time Tony Lawrance had returned to England from his seven-year
chaplaincy at Saugor, to become the rector of Barmston on the Yorkshire
coast, south of Scarborough and Bridlington. Dad continued to tend his
widow's grave at Saugor as long as he was in India.

Was Mum happy? I think so. Although, in her words, she felt *'a fish
out of water'* at times, she suffered such feelings throughout her life. They
were not any stronger while she was involved in the life of the Indian
Army. Most important of all, she laid down many happy memories on
which she would feed for the rest of her life.

Was Dad happy? I am sure he was. You can see it in his face in the
photograph that shows him holding me in his arms outside his bungalow in February 1946, just after we had all arrived in Saugor from
Bombay. I am happy too, held firmly in his strong hands, peaceful and
content in his embrace, as he looks towards Mum (who was taking the
photograph) with a broad, untroubled smile and an unfurrowed brow
(Plate 9).

But now there was a new source of great urgency, straight after the
efforts of the War. Mr Attlee's government announced that the subcontinent would be subjected to partition and that India and Pakistan
would become independent states at the end of 1947. That date was later
brought forward to 15th August of that year. The existing Indian
officers were promoted and others commissioned, so that they would be
ready for an orderly transfer of authority within the Army. Everything
happened in a rush, and there was no time for Dad to take Mum to
Pachmarhi, so she never saw his 'spiritual home in the hills'.

Because of Dad's modesty, Mum probably did not fully take in, at that
time, what he had achieved and contributed to the Army at Saugor in
those years. It was all much too strange for her. Later she understood
better. Nonetheless she was wholly aware of his other qualities, and she

too sensed later on that, after their return to England, he was not always given his due. Many others experienced this on their return Home. Mum always specially liked those who appreciated Dad's modesty and humility, but who also saw beyond these qualities and valued him even more highly for himself and for his achievements.

This fear of Dad's not being valued, for all that he was and did, became an open wound for her later when he was in his fifties and sixties and Huntington's devastated him. Huntington's makes people want to hide themselves, or what has become of them, from others. It makes others not want to know you. See it, and you will understand.

As 1946 and 1947 passed, Dad filled his buff notebooks with preparations for the return to England and with information about the possibility of retirement from the Army.

At the end of 1946, in his last annual report on Dad, Colonel Gray wrote: *'A first class administrative officer. A most conscientious and reliable man in every way. One can thoroughly rely on any work he is given being done most thoroughly and efficiently. Has foresight, imagination and the power of getting good work out of his subordinates. Popular with all ranks, but a strict disciplinarian.'*

Brigadier Cameron, commandant of the Infantry School at Saugor and well known among his contemporaries as a commander of the highest quality, who made great demands on his officers, added this final comment on the last day of December 1946: *'A first class administrative officer who has given unreservedly of his very best in his appointment as admin officer/Infantry Weapons Wing/Infantry school. I entirely agree with his CO's remarks.'*

Both men graded Dad as 'above average' and recommended him for his next promotion. They offered him a regular commission in the British Army back at Home but he decided to take retirement, after twenty eight years as a soldier. In his report in 1946, Colonel Gray records that, in their conversation about what he might do after retiring from the Army, Dad mentioned his interest in *'farming, gardening and social work'*.

Dad began to make detailed lists of all that they had to send back to England. It amounted to enough to fill eight heavy teak boxes, each of them four feet by three feet by three feet in size, which he and Mum would pack, beginning in April 1947, for the journey Home. The luggage would carry the belongings that he had gathered over half a lifetime.

My impact is all too evident: *'wool booties (5 pairs), wool socks (3 pairs), wool gloves (1 pair), baby hat, Christening gown, baby's nightdresses (2), baby's woollen vests (3) … and toy piano and teddy bears.'* But another list includes a *'wooden tray (1)'*, exquisitely carved from walnut for serving tea or coffee; and a *'panther skin, lynx skin (1), cheetah skin rug (1), napkin rings (3)'*, carved delicately from ivory; and, less exotically, a *'trilby hat'*. Then there is a list of presents for both Dad's and Mum's families in England: ivory napkin rings, with penknives for the boys.

On 9th September, Dad entrusted Margo, our bull-terrier, to Kundan. For fifteen or more years he used to send money orders to Kundan and Kalloo when he wrote to them, and, with the help of letter-writers, they used to send him some news of the new India.

We made our way by railway to Bombay. The subcontinent was in turmoil.

On the eighteenth of the month, after spending twenty-five years and six months there – the vast bulk of his adult years and, at that time, well over half his life – Dad left India for ever, sailing with Mum and me from Bombay to England on the liner *Strathnaver*.

☉

Like the Roman centurion who had served in the army so long in Britain that he could not bear the thought of leaving it and returning to Italy as the Roman Empire weakened and retrenched, Dad had loved India.

> *Legate, I come to you in tears – My cohort ordered home!*
> *I've served in Britain forty years. What should I do in Rome?*
> *Here is my heart, my soul, my mind – the only life I know.*
> *I cannot leave it all behind. Command me not to go!*

Now we were gone.

Dad's life could in any case never be the same again; but far worse than that loss, something happened to him on the voyage Home, something that would not be known to me for sixty years.

15

Making a Home

DAD OFTEN SPOKE to me of the horrors of Partition in India.

Some Indians who have exercised a heavy responsibility for their country's government and security over the years since then, sixty years on, have also told me of those terrible days, which trouble their memories as much as they sully the reputation of Mr Attlee's government and that of Lord Mountbatten, the last Viceroy. One of the wisest and most experienced of those Indians told me privately that, had it been possible to grant India her independence a year or two later, much bloodshed would have been avoided.

Dad was not sure that, even in that way, it would have been possible to avoid tens of thousands of deaths. In any case, there was no choice. Great Britain had been bled white by her role in the War. The victors, the Soviet Union and the United States, each had a strong interest in the dissolution of the Empire. They had little care for or understanding of the human consequences for the peoples of India and Pakistan. They wished to divide and share the spoils, Stalin cashing them in for ideology and Roosevelt and Truman for business profits.

For so many who, like Dad, loved the people and their land and had served there for so long, it was a tragedy that the British left the country in such a way.

ℚ

In her notes made fifty years after the events, Mum wrote:

'Arriving in Bombay after a trying journey from Saugor – I was five months pregnant – heat and journey were trying on a troop ship.
Arriving in England – journey down to Plymouth and Plympton – meeting

79

Jack's family and mine again. Eventually obtaining a cottage at Venton, near Sparkwell. Happy times with Jack and John in the cottage.

Going to have Ralf at Horrabridge nursing home. Hilda looked after Jack and John ... Travelled home to Venton cottage and Jack and John.'

©

They called it 'Saugor Cottage'. It was built deep into the left side of the lane which, with its tall Devonshire banks and hedges, runs down from the village of Sparkwell to the hamlet of Venton.

Venton means 'spring' or 'well' in Cornish. Wells and springs can be places of magic, good magic, and so it was there.

And it is here that I have my first memory, as clear as the water of the spring. It is of Dad, wearing a jersey and corduroy trousers, and the trilby hat that returned with us from India in one of the black teak boxes. Dad is carrying two heavy, galvanised buckets down the hill to draw our water from the pump, fed by the spring at the foot of the lane. It is December by now, and there I am, rolling down the hill a few of the logs that Dad has stacked so carefully beside the cottage. Dad fills the buckets and then we walk up the hill together, with my hand held securely, gently in his. Dad puts the buckets down carefully at the gate, and we walk down the hill again. Together we collect the logs and restack them. We do this often together. I love Dad.

Of course there was no electricity, and Mum sometimes cooked with an oven made out of a large biscuit tin standing on two little brick walls, over an open wood fire.

We had an Elsan chemical toilet, the contents of which Dad used to bury each week.

Once a week he travelled into Plymouth to do some shopping. He used to buy fish from the fishermen at the market on the quayside at the Barbican. Perhaps this simple, regular life served to remind him of his boyhood in Newlyn.

Dad used to buy an occasional pint of beer, or a bottle of Forest brown ale, at the Treby Arms in Sparkwell. The pub, with its comforting yellow, nicotine-stained walls, and with the same publican, survived unspoiled and unchanged for forty years. Mr Nelder, with his black moustache, shining bald head and courteous, quiet manner, remembered Dad all those years later. *'He was a gentleman,'* he told me.

In the cottage, oil lamps with dark green or pink shades lighted our two rooms, one up and one down. There was a Claygate brick fireplace downstairs. We had roaring log fires. The cottage has been in ruins for years now, but you can still see the remains of the fireplace in the hedge in the lane.

Two Christmas trees, so tall that they bent over against the ceiling, were surrounded by toys. The postman, delivering parcels, commented to Mum that it looked like an enchanted land. It was.

The rent was only fifteen shillings (75p) a week, because the steep bank of earth supporting a hazel and hawthorn hedge at the back of the cottage were giving way, and it was Dad's responsibility to deal with that problem. He employed Mum's brother Jack, who earned his living as a jobbing gardener, to build a dry-stone wall there.

This was as much an act of generosity on Dad's part as a necessity. Congenial work was hard to find in Plympton. In the tiny notebooks in which Dad, in his beautiful, neat hand, kept his accounts in the 1940s and 1950s, there are entries indicating his occasional subsidy to some member of Mum's family, even after it became necessary for him to manage his money very carefully. I am struck by the extent of his generosity to a few of her relatives, hidden away in these books.

By the middle of January 1948, when my brother was born, the primroses were already flowering in the Devonshire hedges. Mum wrote: *'Our walks, picking flowers and sticks together to light our lovely fire … food rationed and therefore enjoyed more as a treat.'*

At the end of the month my brother was baptised at Sparkwell church, and in February we moved away.

Perhaps through some Army connection, Dad applied for and was appointed to the position of estate manager at Thoresby Hall in Nottinghamshire. It looked a good prospect. Farming and gardening, together with social work, were the occupations he had mentioned as interests for work after retiring from the Army at the time of his final report with Colonel Gray in Saugor. Mum's family on her mother's side had originated in that part of the English Midlands.

As we travelled north in the train, the primroses in the hedgerows gave way to the grime and soot of the industrial Midlands and the coalfields of Nottinghamshire. If Mum had had any romantic feeling about returning to her mother's roots (which is likely: she always maintained that the prettiest women came from Nottingham), they soon disappeared. She hung out the washing in the dark mists of a hard winter and took in the clothes grimy with coal-dust.

The weather was especially harsh for Dad after so many years in the

tropics, with no chance gradually to get used to the temperatures and
the raw dampness in England.

We were living in a flat above the stables, and one day I nearly fell
through the window. The pane of glass that I had knocked out of the
frame hit a woman walking in the yard below. Only her thick hair protected her from a serious injury. Mum wrote:

> 'There were thirty-two stone steps up to our flat, which was like a hospital –
> long passages. It was a converted stables at Thoresby Hall ... We had to share
> the flat with a young lodger who was not a very likeable chap. When we opened
> the window, coal-dust from a nearby mine blew in. Memories of Nottingham
> not good, I'm afraid.'

The single happy memory from that time was when Dad and Mum
took us to Sherwood Forest and we stood inside Robin Hood's 'Major
Oak'. There seems to have been no chance to find a better place to live,
and it is not clear that Dad was enjoying the work.

So Dad and Mum decided to move to Cornwall. For a while, Dad's
pension would be enough for us to live on. They thought that St Ives
would be ideal for the four of us.

Dad travelled down to Penzance by train. He visited Newlyn and
stayed with his family. He found a bungalow, then called 'Maginot', one
and a half miles to the west of the centre of St Ives and eight miles to
the east of Land's End.

It was a long day's journey from Penzance back to the rail-head for
Thoresby Hall at East Retford. Bidding farewell to his sisters, Dad left
Penzance on the 9.45 am train. He arrived at Paddington at 5pm, caught
the 6.05pm at King's Cross, and finally reached East Retford at 9.14pm.

He told Mum the news that there were few houses available at that
time, and he showed her the careful drawings of the bungalow and its
garden that he had made.

Mum was overjoyed about the house and the garden.

We moved to Cornwall in the middle of June and they renamed the
bungalow 'Babworth', the name of a country house, not far from
Thoresby Hall, where Mum's parents had once been in service.

Mum wrote:

> 'The journey to St. Ives via Paddington – Uncle Jack Aldersey and Auntie
> Nellie's present of food for the journey to Cornwall. Travelling first class, under
> Jack's pension arrangements for one year.'

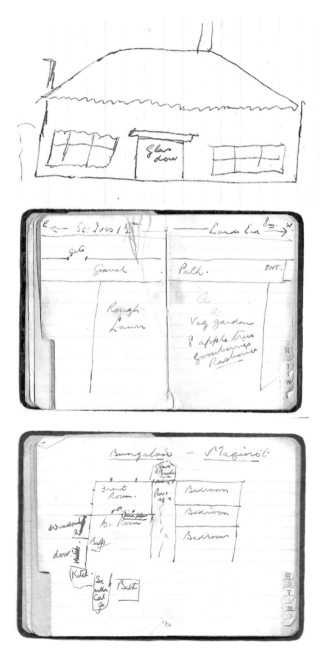

On part of the journey from Paddington we shared a compartment with the Duke of Portland who was shrewd enough to praise 'the boys' to Mum. She always remembered his beautiful leather luggage, inscribed with *KG* after his name, in gold leaf.

For Dad, too, it was a happy return. He was devoted to his sisters, and all his life he felt a special responsibility for his youngest sister, Kathleen, who never married.

The mild climate in west Cornwall was perfect for Dad. Despite his time in India (more than half his life, so far, had been spent in its heat), Dad did not feel the need to wear his blue tweed overcoat at all during our two years at St Ives.

He loved to work in the garden. He kept a few fowls for eggs. I played alongside him. Together we cleaned out the chicken house. I did my best to work with him in the flower garden, pouring water over the granite birdbath and rocks that lined the flowerbeds and watching it mysteriously steam up on the sun-baked stones.

Behind the bungalow was a field where the local farmer grew swedes and cabbages. When Dad and I were there on our side of the hedge, working together in the chicken run, the farmer would pass by on his tractor, which had only recently replaced two heavy shire-horses. On his way home to his midday dinner, he would call out to us, *'See 's af'noon!'*

My first memory of Mum is the image of her cooking pasties in the biscuit-tin oven over an open fire kindled between two rows of bricks in the back garden.

It was a happy time for her, too. She wrote:

'Bonfires in the garden at St. Ives;
cooking in the garden;
times on the beach, building sandcastles;
visits from all the family, and walking over the cliffs and climbing down to the
  sea and being among the rocks;
lovely picnics at a sort of tor quite near our bungalow'

– 'the Reocks', as I used to call them.

Many parents say that their happiest years are the first few years of their children's lives. Of course, Ralf and I were happy too. There is a photograph of all four of us at a picnic on the cliffs in the summer sunshine. In front of us, clearly visible and legible, is a Weetabix cereal box. So full of happiness and health is the picture that Wally (who took the snap, and loved to eat Weetabix and honey for breakfast) suggested that the company should use it as an advertisement: *'If Weetabix can make people as fit and happy as that, you should try it!'*

Dad was planning our future. He knew the value of schools and learning. I feel it when I dip into the books that he gathered over the years in India, especially the set texts, anthologies and grammars that he used when, in the early 1930s, he studied for his Higher National Certificate.

The photograph that Florence Louisa gave him for his fourteenth birthday shows him and his fellow pupils, some sitting and some standing, in well-ordered rows in front of their classroom. The school looks neat and tidy, well run and careful of its pupils, but it was small and limited in what it could offer them.

Schools in west Cornwall had not changed much in forty or fifty years. Dad felt it would be best to move to Plympton, which had a good grammar school. Florrie's children had attended it; in fact, they had shown it to Dad when its new building was being constructed during his home leave in 1936. Then, there were other good schools in Plymouth, twenty-five minutes away by bus.

Dad also knew that he must get a job to provide us with an adequate income. This would be easier near Plymouth. The post-war inflation was already eating into his precious pension and savings.

Dad went to Plympton for a few days and lodged there with Hilda and Fred. With their help, Dad found a house. It was in a quiet road, lined with lime trees and lilac bushes. Behind it stretched a lush green field, safe and open for children to play.

The house, no. 10 Moorland Road, was only fifty yards from the high street, called Ridgeway. It was ideally placed in the village, on the bus route to Plymouth, near the shops, the library, the primary school and the doctor's surgery.

No. 10 was part of a mid-Victorian terrace, built in 1867, with a secluded walled back garden. The front garden and the sitting-room faced west.

Before we moved in, Dad arranged for a Rayburn to be installed in the kitchen, for cooking and hot water, and for the bathroom to be fitted out afresh.

On a damp, drizzly, rather muggy day in August 1950, we left St Ives. We said a sad goodbye to Miss Date, the local shopkeeper, who gave us home-made pasties, wrapped in white napkins, to eat on the train. *'She is an honest, kind woman,'* Bernard Leach, the potter, had told Dad when we had moved in. His studio was just down the road from 'Babworth'.

Mrs Stone, our next-door neighbour, who was regarded locally as a Cornish witch and was known to everyone as 'Lovejoy' because of her sour temperament, was less friendly. On the day we left she flew a Union Jack, left over from the VE Day celebrations or, perhaps, from Princess Elizabeth's marriage to the Duke of Edinburgh in 1947, in order to express her joy at the departure of two noisy young boys who played raucously in the garden next to hers.

Ralf and I stood on the platform of St Ives station with our luggage: each of us had a small suitcase. I wore a navy gabardine mackintosh and a cap. We passed through damp, misty countryside, eating Miss Date's pasties. Nearly three hours later we rolled across Brunel's bridge over the River Tamar and entered Devon. We skirted the dockyard at Devonport. There were glimpses of some of the ships of the Royal Navy, and then of the city of Plymouth, still in ruins from the blitz.

The people of Plymouth were mainly from the working and lower middle classes, labourers and skilled artisans, many of whom worked in the dockyard. There was a thin crust of professional middle class people. Some of them were from families which had lived there for several generations. Others had come to Plymouth early in their careers, perhaps as schoolmasters or doctors, and had stayed on there for the rest of their lives, in love with the sea, the countryside and Dartmoor, and the native Devonians, with their kindness and relaxed way of life. A tiny number of institutions served this professional group, including one famously good restaurant (Pedro's) and the Plymouth Proprietary Library.

1 William, Dad's father, c.1910   2 Florence Louisa, Dad's mother, 1914

3 Dad's school-leaving photograph, 1915
He is standing on the teacher's left

4 In mourning together, after
William's death, November 1914

5 Dad in Ireland, 1920

6 Promoted Sergeant, India, 1935

7 Commissioned, and by now a Major,
1943

8 Married, December 1944

9 Outside Dad's bungalow, Saugor, February 1946

10 The bungalow in Saugor, my parents' first home together

11 Plympton,
Devon, 1953

12 The two of
them together,
23 April 1966

There was at that time one seedy area, Union Street, but everywhere else reigned respectability, gentleness and harmony. You would not believe it now. As a child, I could sense this serene calm and could feel that the houses, streets and gardens were prized and somehow loved by the Plymothians. Of course, I had no idea that this was an unusual time. I did not then understand that the people sincerely treasured them as relics, spared by the still recent fall of bombs. This gratitude for life and peace in the city lasted perhaps another ten years, until 1960. It seems to have been something like that in most of the country.

We caught a taxi to no. 10 from North Road station in Plymouth, although at that date there was still a station in Plympton. Dad opened the green, wooden gate into the garden, protected from no. 12 and the road by a privet hedge. There was no hedge between the small, adjoining lawns in front of no. 10 and no. 8.

With a Yale key, unchanged in all our years there, Dad unlocked the heavy green front door and led us into a lobby, the inner door of which was glazed with Victorian glass panes – blue, green, dark yellow and red – through which the setting sun would cast its peaceful light, like a spell, on us for fifty years. He opened the glass door, and we were in a long passage, rather shabbily decorated with fawn wallpaper, but graced by an elegant banister and staircase. On the right was a large sitting-room, with a bay window looking on to the front garden, and a dining-room with a tall window giving on to a slate path leading to the back garden. Both rooms had tall, marble fireplaces – white in the sitting-room, black in the dining-room.

We walked along the passage to the kitchen and scullery, beyond a small lobby with a door designed to allow the Victorian proprietors to enter the garden without passing through the kitchen and scullery, the domain of their servants. When the house was built, there would probably have been a cook and a housemaid working there, the sort of work done by Mum's mother in her first years in service.

Together we explored the rooms upstairs. There were three bedrooms, a dressing-room next to the front bedroom, and a bathroom. The bathroom and back bedroom, the kitchen and scullery below them, with a larder and coal cellar, formed a tenement jutting out into the back garden, which was bordered by a stone wall six feet high. A wooden door led into the back lane. The garden was dominated by a lilac bush, big enough for us to make a primitive tree house, and an enormous 'New Dawn' rose-bush.

In September Dad set about finding a job. At the same time, I started school in the infants' class, in the room in which Mum had herself begun to attend lessons a few weeks after the outbreak of the First World War.

We owned no. 10 for fifty years.

These decisions and plans turned out to be Dad's last, great initiatives for us all. Everything depended on them, and they successfully set the pattern of our lives for so long.

Only now do I know how costly they must have been, how draining of his mental resources. For, hidden from him and us, within every cell of Dad's body, things were on the move.

16

'Huntington's explains it all'

IT BEGAN with Kathleen.

Before the War, Kathleen had lived with Clara and Charlie. So when, at the end of her war-work in the aircraft factory in Gloucestershire, she moved back to Newlyn, it was Nora's turn to give her a home. For some years she lodged with Nora and Reg and their six sons.

Kathleen began to work at a guesthouse in Penzance, and often brought home some of the unused food that was going to waste at the end of the day. Nora's sons remember the treats that Kathleen brought them, like trifles and fruit salad. In those days, in the late 1940s, food rationing was even more severe in Great Britain than it had been during the war. Despite that, we continued to send supplies to Germany where the population was on the verge of starvation.

It was in the late 1940s that Kathleen began to be affected: chromosome 4, gene IT15.

'She got the shakes and jitters,' one of Nora's sons told me. *'We laughed at her.'*

And across all the time that has passed since those days, now nearly sixty years, you can hear the shame and guilt and confusion and embarrassment in his voice.

'We didn't understand,' he told me. *'We were too young.'*

And how could they possibly understand? How could they know? For Kathleen was the first in her generation to be affected. All of Nora's six sons had been born long after her uncle Frank had died of Huntington's chorea in 1921. Not one of them had seen it. How could they know or guess?

After Dad's death in 1972 I began to be troubled about Auntie Kath. Had I been unkind to her? Had I made things worse for her? Had I made Dad unhappy by doing anything that upset her?

Just before Christmas in 1975 I wrote to Mum about it and discussed it with her on the telephone. On what would have been her thirty-first wedding anniversary she wrote me a letter about my fears in unusually direct terms.

> *'You are wrong about Auntie Kath. She came to us at every Christmas and for a month at St Ives once, and many times besides. Do not worry yourself on that account. I was extremely fond of Auntie Kath and as far as possible did what I could. None of us are angels – if I ever did anything wrong may God also forgive me. Every Sunday she had her nice bath and tea here, and I know that she enjoyed it.*
>
> *You and Ralf were lovely to Kath whenever she came and she had great joy from your company … So please do not be worried about that which did not happen.'*

Huntington's is a disease of families, even happy ones, as well as of individuals.

A couple of years after Kathleen became ill, Clara's health began to go down hill as she slowly developed the first symptoms.

Clara's last surviving child, Barbara, has seen more of Huntington's than anyone should. Her three sisters and her brother developed the disease and died of it.

Barbara recalls that, at around the age of ten, in 1952, she first became aware, and consciously took in, that something strange was happening to her mother. In order to make up for the loss of what her mother could give her, in attention and closeness, she somehow began to *'move over'*, as she puts it, to her father, so as to draw from him more of what all ten-year-olds need from their parents. Later she came to understand that, at that age, she had to protect herself by distancing herself from all that was happening to her mother.

There is something about the drop in energy and interest, the look of 'lostness' caused by Huntington's, that drives a child to do this, just to survive the pain of that feeling of loss. It happens; it is bound to happen. We were lucky to have two parents. Imagine what it would be like in a one-parent family. I dare not. God forbid.

And Dad was living there at St Ives with us, near Newlyn, from 1948 to 1950, as this began to happen to Kathleen and Clara.

Dad had known his Uncle Frank. He must surely have learnt some-thing of how his life had ended, although he was away from Newlyn during his last two years and, if you have not been involved in Hunt-ington's, you will hardly believe how far we will go to hide the truth from ourselves and from those whom we love and want to protect. Florrie and Nora are likely to have known how Uncle Frank had died and probably they saw him in his last, most affected years. The other sisters were, perhaps, too young in 1921 to take it in, especially if Frank was being protected and kept out of view.

So when Dad saw what was happening to Kathleen and, a little later, to Clara, something would have stirred in his memory.

Once you have seen it, you never forget it.

What Dad made of it, who can tell? Certainly he could have had no idea of its real significance. Ninety five per cent of the doctors in the country were ignorant of that in 1950. But I suspect that some ill-defined anxiety crept into his mind. If so, was it an ordinary anxiety Dad felt, or was there already something more at work?

A couple of months before we moved from St Ives to Plympton, Florrie's son Terry and his fiancée Maureen, both in their early twenties, stayed with us for a week's holiday. It was June 1950, Terry told me. What difficulty Dad and Mum had in handling their two young sons, they thought. Perhaps it was just the trials of middle-aged parents, now forty-eight and forty years old, dealing with the energy of a four-year-old and a two-year-old, but Terry and Maureen were puzzled. Whether or not because of this experience, they settled for one child. But when, not long afterwards, he next saw Dad in the very early 1950s, Terry recalls a hesitancy in him, a nervousness and lack of confidence. His behaviour and manner were strikingly different from what he remembered of Dad at the time of his Home leave in 1936 and 1944, and completely at odds with everything in the detailed reports on Dad's confident manner and efficient work, written just four years earlier in India.

There is another witness to what was happening. At the wedding reception held at no. 7 Stone Barton after Dad and Mum were married in 1944, Terry had been joined by Hilda's son, John, to sing some songs. Mum accompanied them at the piano. John did not see Dad again for six years.

John was fifteen years old at the time of the wedding. He has a vivid recollection of Dad at that time: very smart, with an upright bearing, clearly a military man, who spoke briefly and to the point. His description matches Dad's reports.

John left the grammar school at seventeen, in 1946, and he worked for a few months as a cub reporter on the local newspaper, the South Devon Times. Sixty years later he still had his reporter's eye, an objectivity and cool detachment. He was away from Devon on National Service between mid-1947 and May 1949. He then lived in his parents' home in Plympton and worked at a sports shop in Plymouth until January 1951, when he moved to Southampton to work for the Ordnance Survey. Soon after that he went into business and made a great success of his career.

For nearly six years, then, John did not see Dad. He met him again in Plympton in the spring of 1950 when Dad went to stay with Hilda and Fred for a few days while he was searching for a house for us to live in after our move from St Ives.

Immediately, John noticed a difference. Dad's speech was a little vague; his bearing was less upright and less military; he seemed somehow to have less control of the movements of his limbs and had begun to stumble and to drop things. At first, during those months in 1950, John thought that the reason for this change was that Dad was finding it difficult to adapt to life in England after spending so long in the Army in India. After all, it was bound to be a difficult change. Of course, John had never met Kathleen or Clara, so he had no reason to suspect that there was 'something in the family'.

John recalls that he talked about Dad with his parents at the end of 1950, in the weeks before he moved to Southampton. *'We were aware of something, but we didn't mention it to anyone else. We noticed that he was rather clumsy around the house. We thought he was missing the ordered life of the Army after so long.'*

But somehow, even at the time, it seemed to John to be more significant than that. Dad was not as incisive as he had been; he was in some way *'bewildered'*. And, with hindsight, John can see that what he was witnessing was the beginning of the slow development of Huntington's disease.

'That explains it all', John said. *'It was the missing piece of the jigsaw. It makes sense of everything else; of all the things that we could explain away on their own and put down to the effects of India or premature ageing because of the hot climate, or a lack of practical dexterity, or late fatherhood ...*

'Huntington's explains it all.'

For a while, after John told me of his memories of 1950, it seemed that there was no one to tell me more of what happened in those years, no one who had been old enough at the time to see what was happening and was still alive with reliable memories.

Then, not long after the death of my cousin Mavis,* I telephoned her brother Gerald, who had by then lived in Canada for over thirty years. Mum had told me that he was a most interesting and kind person, and that she always enjoyed seeing him and talking to him on his visits from Canada.

Gerald had served in the army in India at the end of the Second World War, from 1944 to 1947. He read widely and was well informed about many things. He was blessed with the powerful memory for places and people that seems to come down the line of the Aldersey family, through Mum's mother.

Gerald told me that he had vivid memories of his only meeting with Dad. He had visited us at Venton Cottage in his Morris Cowley motor car only a month or so after we arrived back from India. He had been demobilised in April 1947 and had used his 'demob' money to buy a car, first an Austin Seven and then the Morris. He was twenty-one years old.

It was the autumn, probably late October or early November. The evenings were drawing in. Gerald had taken his mother, Edie, out for a drive in the country that afternoon and Edie had pointed out to him the signpost to the hamlet of Venton. Gerald had suggested that they call in on us. Edie warned him, *'You may get a surprise when you see your Uncle Jack.'* Gerald did not understand what to make of this.

It was a lovely visit, Gerald told me. He parked in the narrow lane outside the cottage. While Mum and Edie were talking separately and I was playing on the carpet, he had an interesting talk with Dad about India, part of it in Urdu. Gerald had visited Peshawar, Razmak, Meerut, Rawal Pindi, Derha Dun, Poona and Bihar before being moved to Siam (Thailand). He and Edie stayed with us for a couple of hours.

Gerald's work took him away from home a good deal, and then he emigrated, so he never met Dad again.

Gerald recalls that perhaps as many as a dozen times during the visit, Dad was affected by *'spasms'*. As he sat in a big armchair, one of his shoulders or the other would inexplicably jerk upwards; one of his feet

---

* Mavis was the second daughter of Mum's sister Edie.

would leap a little from the floor by about three or four inches. Two or three times his body leant or twitched forward and back.

The first symptom that he noticed stuck clearly in Gerald's memory. Dad's right arm rose suddenly above his shoulder, *'in the way children raise their hands in class to ask for permission to go out of the room to the toilet'*. When this happened, Gerald jerked back into his own chair in surprise and he was afraid that this reflex reaction might have offended Dad. He began to feel that Dad was aware of what was happening and felt that Gerald was *'staring at him'*. Gerald was confused by what he saw and did not quite know how to behave. But Dad took a lot of interest in him and they had a good conversation.

Gerald told me that it was terrible to see someone so intelligent afflicted in this way, so soon after he had been fit and well at the wedding (according to Edie) less than three years earlier. He thought that it must be something like Parkinson's disease, and knew nothing of Huntington's.

On the way home in the car, Edie *'had a good cry'*. *'Grace is such a lovely girl, and she has got a marvellous constitution and she is coping better than I expected.'* Edie dried her tears because she did not wish her husband Len to see that she had been crying.

Gerald has no idea who it was who had already seen Dad and had been able to warn Edie about the change in his health since the wedding. He remembers that he heard a little later, perhaps from Edie or Len, that *'something had happened'* when we were at sea on the journey back from India in September 1947, and that Mum had had to call for medical help for Dad. Gerald wondered whether, suddenly and out of the blue, Dad had suffered his first *'spasm'* during the sea voyage.

Who can tell, but it seems possible that it was on board ship, as he was returning to England to settle at Home after his twenty-five years' service in India, that Huntington's began to take its grip on Dad.

Whatever the truth of that, Mum wrote to me:

'There were so many happy times and memories at Venton and St Ives and no. 10 Moorland Road.'

17
Number 10

WE SETTLED into no. 10.

On a Monday morning at the beginning of September 1950, Mum took me by the hand and, together, we walked down Station Hill for my first day's school. In the walls on both sides of the road grew pink valerian flowers and ferns, some light green, others like dark green lace.

The door opened on to the infants' class of Plympton County Primary School. The building was still rather battered from its service in the War as a government office, a little dark and forbidding with high ceilings and tall, narrow windows. Mrs Gardiner, the teacher, used to open them with an S-shaped brass hook fixed to the end of a long, wooden pole. She saw that I was subdued on my first morning at school, and she gave me a duster to clean and tidy a shelf. The atmosphere was peaceful, friendly and warm.

'He'll be all right,' Mrs Gardiner told Mum. Soon I was more than all right. I began to love school and learning, soaking up information and thoughts and impressions.

Mum began to work on making our new home. This is how she remembered it:

'Taking the little boys to the babies' school at the bottom of Station Hill and Mrs Gardiner.

Lovely times playing the games we bought for their birthdays; table tennis. Fireworks on Guy Fawkes' day – visits to Lee Moor to fire the big rockets. Walks with the old push chair to Cadover Bridge. Trips in the train from Plympton station to Paignton zoo. Trips on the train to Princetown from Marsh Mills – picking whortleberries and mushrooms. One game – on the stairs

95

playing buses, with John and Ralf, driver and conductor, and Dad and me
passengers!

Lovely books Dad bought for them and reading stories. Parties in the dining
room with lots of food on the big table. They had great times in the back garden,
building a house in the corner and lighting a fire.

Our visits to Mrs Barnard's shop in Ridgeway to buy little toys and games.'

Dad got a job. With the advice and encouragement of one of his
friends from India, he was interviewed and selected to become a
member of the War Office Constabulary, now known as the Ministry of
Defence Police.

Dad was sworn in as a constable by Superintendent Hill during his
training course at Didcot. He became PC 1484. While he was in training at Didcot Dad visited Uncle Jack and Auntie Nellie in London. He
sent us cards and presents – for Ralf and me, bright red toy telephones.

After the month's training at Didcot, Dad came home and began to
work at 'Coypool', a munitions factory and depot at Marsh Mills, about
midway between Plympton and Plymouth.

His wages for the first week in January 1951 were £6 2s 6d (£6.12½p),
net of tax and other deductions. He worked a six-day week, with 24
days' leave (four weeks) a year. It was shift work, rotating week by week
from early turn (6am to 2pm), to late turn (2pm to 10pm), and finally
night duty (10pm to 6am). One week in three he had to catch up with
his sleep during the day.

Quite often Dad had to work on Sundays. Occasionally he had a long
weekend off duty, from 2pm on Friday to 10pm on Monday. But, as
the notes that he made during the course at Didcot record, *'There is*
also a short weekend (from 6 o'clock on Sunday morning until 10 o'clock the
same evening) which we shall not go too deeply into,' in Superintendent Hill's
words.

The daily and weekly pattern of Dad's work established itself. It lasted
twelve years.

$$\mathbb{Q}$$

Month by month in those years Dad kept an account of our income and
expenditure. From his childhood he had learnt how to budget.

In his last years in India his fellow officers entrusted to him the
handling of their mess-chits and bills. *'It was his integrity we trusted',* one
of them (a great drinker) told me.

Dad did the same for St Peter's church, Saugor, as church secretary and treasurer. Among the last cheques he signed in India was one for the church's quota assessment, to be paid to the Nagpur diocesan treasurer – 500 rupees, dated 3rd June 1947; and for 176 rupees he bought from the Saugor Mission one brown and two red rugs. The rugs remained in our dining room until we sold no. 10, in November 2000.

Dad lived by his maxim, *'Take care of the pennies and the pounds will take care of themselves.'* He was generous, but he knew, and taught me, that *'a fool and his money are soon parted'. 'Rupees – annas – paise,'* he used to say to me, like a mantra. How urgent was his concern to provide for us.

Our budget was small. It was not helped by the condition of the house, which the previous owner had let run down. No. 10 often needed to be patched up, and Hilda recommended a builder from Plymouth, Mr Easterbrook, who was poor at his work and who over-charged for what he did. As soon as Mr Cosh, a local builder, and Mr Foale, the local painter and decorator, had replaced Easterbrook, things improved.

From the neat columns of figures in Dad's small leather-bound account book, it is easy to see that he was carefully managing the budget to put aside money for our education later on. He and Mum succeeded in doing this by spending almost nothing on themselves.

In 1952 Dad's monthly income was about £30 from his Indian Army pension and a little less from his current work. He paid about £10 a month income tax and national insurance contributions, leaving a net income of about £600 a year. The records seem to suggest that Dad also paid a small amount of Indian income tax on his Army pension until the end of March 1955. His gifts of money, by postal order, to Kalloo and Kundan at Saugor, continued for long after that, accompanied by letters giving news of our life in England, to which they replied, using the services of a letter writer. Sitting in the armchair in the dining room, Dad used to read me their letters and tell me stories about their time with him and how they would be living now.

The net figure for his income may have risen to about £750 a year by 1963, when Dad retired. Of course, after his retirement it diminished dramatically. Mum said, *'We'll have to draw in our horns.'*

In July that year, Mum's brother Wally nosily asked him, in my presence, about his income. We were just beginning the painful process of adjusting to living on Dad's Indian and War Office pensions. Wally asked Dad about his income before retirement, and Dad told him that it had never exceeded £1,000 a year. Wally seemed taken aback or perplexed by the answer, and that wordless response of his was a tribute to how Dad and Mum managed.

Dad's planning, and his and Mum's self-denial (like Dad's tanners from coal-heaving as a boy), saved us and, in truth, created much joy and happiness for the four of us.

ℚ

Our daily happiness, at tea-time after school, was focused on 'Children's Hour' on the BBC Home Service.

> *'Between the dark and the daylight,*
> *When the night is beginning to lower,*
> *Comes a pause in the day's occupations,*
> *That is known as the Children's Hour.'*

As Mum recorded:

> *'Listening to Children's Hour, with Uncle Mac, and David Davis and Violet Carson and Herbert Smith ... Wonderful serials and stories from our black Vidor radio set, by the Rayburn in the kitchen in winter and in summer out on the rickety table in the back garden at teatime.'*

Our annual happiness was centred on our caravan holiday. This became a tradition. It began in 1952 and lasted for fourteen summers.

Dad heard about Challaborough, a big sandy beach near Bigbury-on-Sea and Burgh Island in south Devon, from Mr Pascoe, a colleague at work. Mr Pascoe owned a caravan there and was willing to let it to us. In 1952 Dad paid him £5 for two weeks' rent of the caravan, and £3 to Mr Jeffrey, the owner of the local garage and taxi firm, to take us the thirty miles there and to bring us home in his black taxi, a comfortable pre-war Morris Ten. The car seats were upholstered in sagging dark blue leather and the car's huge chrome headlamps stood like pudding basins balanced on their sides on the front mud-guards.

In that first year there were only a dozen to twenty caravans at Challaborough, all parked to the west of the little stream that runs down the valley into the bay. This land belonged to the Crooks family, who had lived nearby for many years.

Mr Crooks also ran a small shop that sold bread and milk, newspapers and groceries, and a tiny café where Dad bought us wonderful milkshakes for 6d (2½p). Ralf and I would take it in turns to go with Dad to the shop and café for this treat. For many years we could buy all our daily food with a ten-shilling note (50p).

Our caravan had plenty of ground to itself and a small garden, with a mountain ash tree. It was close to the stream that flowed quick and clear, bordered by sedge and reeds at its mouth. We lived there, the four of us, happily and peacefully for a fortnight.

We specially loved the weeks that we sometimes spent at the caravan at the end of August, stretching into the first few days of September, when the shadows lengthened after teatime and we swam late in the day. By 6 o'clock the tide had washed the sands clean and smooth and all was quiet; not that there was litter or many people holidaying there in the early days.

Sometimes we used to walk over the cliffs to Bigbury-on-Sea to the east, where Mum loved to play the penny-in-the-slot-machines, or to Ayrmer Cove, which we called the 'Magic Beach', to the west. But, apart from those outings, we felt no reason to leave the caravan site and the beach until Mr Jeffrey arrived to take us back to no.10, where we always remarked how long and green the front lawn had grown in our absence.

In August 1952 Dad made a note in his accounts that he spent £3 on 'Fred: taxi'. It was the start of another annual ritual.

Uncle Fred, with Auntie Hilda, would take us for a day's tour of beauty spots on Dartmoor. Mum packed our wicker hamper with Cornish pasties and apple pasties, to be slit open and filled with clotted cream. We stopped, often at Dartmeet, for our midday picnic. Later, at teatime, Dad and Fred (whose love of dark brown tea was legendary) would cut out a sod of turf and make a bracken fire to boil the kettle and brew up.

The cars that Dad hired were magnificent Morrises or Austins from the 1930s; always they were black or dark blue. They held all six of us comfortably, with two of us sitting on the folding seats immediately behind the glass screen that separated the driver from the passengers. Ralf and I sometimes took it in turns to sit in front, next to Uncle Fred. We felt very grown up doing this.

Mum wrote:

'One day Andrew White [an only child, whose family lived at no. 6, two doors away from us in the terrace] *was here, and as we loaded into the car and were squashed together with baskets of picnic food, he said 'Lucky pigs!' We could not squeeze anyone else into the car. It was strange, as when Andrew went in their car, a Morris Minor traveller, there was plenty of room; he seemed to want very badly to be jammed in with us.'*

Together with his parents and his grandmother (known as 'Gran-Min'), Andrew and other children used to join us every Guy Fawkes night for our bonfire party in the back garden. Dad was in charge of the fire, and Mum would cook sausages and bake potatoes in the oven of the Rayburn. In the golden red light of the fire Dad would fork up pieces of flaming wood that fell out onto the path, and 'Gran-Min' and some of the other adults used to sit on a bench by our coal cellar. When I met her, long after Dad's death, 'Nobby' Clark's daughter Georgina told me that Dad and Mum gave popular parties at their bungalow in Saugor. Each year, on 5th November, I saw a trace of that, the most sociable and exciting evening of the year.

❦

In the early-1950s the Irish Republican Army waged a short and unsuccessful war of violence and terror in Great Britain. Coypool was an obvious target, and all the police officers were authorised to carry firearms. Dad was then still well enough to do so. He had been a brilliant shot in India, and only took to wearing reading glasses later in the 1950s. For some time he was able to cycle to work, but in 1953 he gave his bicycle to Uncle Charlie. From then he caught the number 21 bus to Coypool. Come rain or snow, he made that journey at all hours of day and night, until 1963.

Often I have wondered how Dad accepted the reduction in his level of responsibility. In India he had been accountable to the Brigadier for running the administration of the infantry weapons school. He had flourished. How did he now manage to find the grace to work under men who were often less educated and cultivated than himself? In fact, he enjoyed the company of his colleagues, all kindly men, many of them of his own age. He found a wry amusement in observing them, as well as enjoying good companionship there. I now understand that this regular work gave Dad a strong framework for life at the time when his confidence and intellectual powers were under attack and gradually, very slowly at first, he was losing the steadiness and coordination of his limbs. One sergeant was a bully, but Dad coped with him, and that man was posted away.

It was Mum who, almost not knowing what she was implying, occasionally seemed to hint that this was all a sacrifice that Dad was willing to make for the three of us. From Dad there was no word of it.

18

At Risk

IN THE SUMMER of 1953 Mum became ill. It seemed impossible. Mum wrote:

'We had not been living long at no.10. I was working quite hard with two small boys and the house to look after. I had 'housewife's tiredness' and my legs were very swollen. Four doctors felt them and said that I must have three or four days in bed.

It was summer time and the children were playing outside the house, in the garden. I was lying in bed with the windows wide open.

Jack had time off to look after me. He used to bring me plates of meat and salad. The lady doctor said, 'Surely you are not going to eat all that?' Jack was so kind, and took great care of John and Ralf. The boys were good, and I had a good time reading Pride and Prejudice.'

Only a little earlier, at the time of the Queen's Coronation on 2nd June, Mum had still been in good health. There is a photograph, snapped on that day by one of Mum's friends, which she always kept in her handbag. It shows her looking bright and cheerful, and catches her face animated, with eyebrows raised and mouth half open in conversation. She found this silly look very amusing and always spoke of that day with great happiness.

After early-morning rain the sun broke through brilliantly in time for the tea and cakes (which Mum had helped to bake) and for the races, games and maypole. Dad was there. I remember how proud he and Mum were of our part in the games and the maypole dance, in which all the local children were involved and for which the boys wore white shirts and blue or red sashes, and the girls white dresses, specially bought or made for that day. There was cheerful, stirring music from a band conducted by Mr Howe, the director of the pit orchestra of the Palace Theatre, Plymouth. His daughter Sheila was in my class at school. It was a great celebration.

Such a day stays with children and helps form them.

It gave me a curious stab of joy on 21st April 2006 to set a small Union Jack in the front window of our house to mark the Queen's eightieth birthday. All the memories and feelings of Coronation Day flooded back to me.

I pondered the words attributed to her mother when the Queen, then only ten years old, discovered how much her life would be changed by her father's accession to the throne as King George the Sixth: *'We must make the best of it.'* It is good advice, as wise for the one who will inherit the Crown as for those at risk from Huntington's. At a difficult time, Mum said to me *'Let's pretend that we are enjoying it, and that will help us do so.'* Perhaps it comes to the same thing.

What was this *'housewife's tiredness'* that overtook Mum so soon after Coronation Day?

A few years after her death, Dr Price, Mum's GP at the end of her life, showed me her medical records. He settled me in a little office in the corner of the surgery, and I made my way through the packet of folded papers. Dad's notes had been destroyed by then, so I never saw them.

The notes showed that Mum suffered from catarrh in mid-June and was prescribed codeine linctus. She must have felt seriously ill, because she always did everything she could to avoid visiting the doctor and she was suspicious of all 'tablets'. A month later she was diagnosed as suffering from oedema (dropsy) of the ankles. Her blood pressure was high (180/120) and there was concern for her kidneys – her blood-urea level was 24mg. By the end of the month the oedema was slight and it had disappeared by 6th August when we were able to go to the caravan for our holiday. While on holiday Mum developed curious sores on the palms of her hands, and it was only at the beginning of November that her hands were said in the notes to be *'almost cured'*.

Mum had not seen a doctor between her second confinement, in January 1948, and mid-1953. She then consulted no doctor between 1953 and 1962, when for two months she had trouble with her varicose veins. So rarely did she visit the surgery that the doctors (Dr Owen and, later, Dr Price) used to tease her about it.

'Give her some Green Shield stamps,' Dr Price called out to his receptionist one day when Mum was over eighty and had reluctantly visited the
surgery.

So ignorant was Mum of the arcane procedures of the National
Health Service that, for a while, she sat patiently in the waiting room,
believing that she had to collect stamps of some sort.

'What are you doing here, Mrs Symons', Dr Price said to her ten minutes
later as he came out of his consulting-room and found her still sitting
there.

'I'm waiting for my Green Shield stamps,' Mum replied, and then
suddenly she saw the joke.

She and Dr Price never forgot this incident – *'foolish woman',* she used
to say of her mistake, and she often told the story against herself to keep
up her spirits in her last years, when even she could no longer avoid
doctors.

I feel sure that Mum became ill in 1953, and was so run down during
the second half of the year, partly because it was in these months that
she understood more fully the seriousness of what was happening to
Dad. She went through some sort of internal crisis.

In those days Kathleen was living in lodgings in the neighbouring
village of Plympton St Maurice, about a mile from us at no.10. Plympton St Maurice and Plympton St Mary are linked by an ancient footpath,
known as the 'Pathfields', shaded by an avenue of tall lime trees planted
in 1897 to commemorate Queen Victoria's Diamond Jubilee. Every
Sunday afternoon, Auntie Kath used to walk over to us, through the
Pathfields, for tea. She used to take a weekly bath in our comfortable
bathroom, supplied with limitless hot water by the Rayburn.

To my shame, I began to find her visits awkward as time passed. Now
I understand how that happened. Gradually, Kathleen's unpredictable,
irrational, choreic movements were becoming pronounced. I did not
laugh at them as Nora's sons who were older than me did, but the movements disturbed me, although I was not consciously aware of what it
was that was troubling me. But for Mum, it was worse. She must have
sensed, to some degree, that Dad was on the same journey as Kathleen,
ten years behind her, and that there could be no turning back.

How long was it before Dad realised that something horrifying was
happening to him?

With all my heart, I hope that somehow Dad and Mum were protected from this knowledge, that it was years before they came to see

the truth, but I cannot believe that it was so. Over the next two or three years they surely realised something more of the true situation.

The mind takes extreme steps to conceal from us what it wishes to ignore, but eventually it surrenders to the truth. That is my experience, but not only mine. Dad was intelligent, observant and sensitive to other people and to atmosphere. He had been only five years old when his grandfather died; and he had been twenty, and away serving in the Army in Ireland, when his Uncle Frank reached the end of his life. The mind could easily push those events aside when Dad had so much to do that occupied and exhausted him, simply in order to earn his living, to survive and to help ensure that his frail mother and his sisters survived.

But now Kathleen and Clara were slowly changing. And above all, I fear, there was the look on the faces of the rest of the family, however much they tried to control their reactions when they were with him. Their expressions, as time passed, must have confirmed to Dad the meaning of the loss of energy, the ebbing of interest, the 'bewilderment' from which he was beginning to suffer.

And what did he read in Mum's face? What did they say to each other?

In Mum's heart, surely, there came to be a fear, a dread, a growing conviction that she was losing Dad, inch by inch, day by day, and she could have had no idea of how or when it would end. My cousin Barbara tells me that she grieved almost more for the loss suffered by her father, Charlie, than for the terrible affliction of Huntington's that her mother, Clara, endured.

Then, for Dad and Mum, there was the horror of what all this might mean for their children. That was with them every moment of the day, and sometimes, I expect, in their dreams.

I feel sure that it was at that time, in mid-1953, that Mum began to see the similarity between Kathleen's advancing affliction and Dad's state, although it was much less pronounced. If you are a member of an affected family and live every hour with a person suffering from Huntington's disease, those movements are unmistakable and terrifying. When, years later, out of the blue, you catch a glimpse of a sufferer out of the corner of your eye on a bus or a train, it is enough to tell you what is happening and you feel the blood run cold. What you feel for the affected person and anyone travelling with them – respect, pity, admiration for their coming out into the world – cannot be described.

Mum's physical constitution was robust. Even at the age of eighty-three she was described by a vascular surgeon as 'remarkably sprightly' as well as 'a delightful elderly lady, and happy in herself'. Dr Price, at the same time, referred to Mum's 'remarkable independence of spirit'. That is why I suspect that it was more than a physical cause that made Mum ill in 1953, when she was only forty-three years old.

What her two young nephews Gerald and John had successively seen, at its very beginning in November 1947 and then in early 1950, Mum now interpreted for the first time for what it was. She could no longer pretend it was not happening or was not significant. The horror of what she saw and sensed would be the outcome for Dad, and what she feared for their sons, worked its way through her system. The shock made her vulnerable to sickness and led to the oedema and her hand infection.

Somehow Mum came to terms with what was happening. She regained her health by the end of the year.

$$\mathbb{Q}$$

Of course, I knew nothing of this threat.

We still enjoyed life, the four of us as a family, in those years. Dad took us to *Oklahoma!* and to *Rosemarie* at the Palace Theatre. We were all thrilled by the colour films of the conquest of Mt. Everest and of the Coronation, which we saw at the Royal cinema soon after those great events. We listened to *South Pacific* together on the radio one Saturday evening. We went on outings to Cadover Bridge and Princetown and Paignton Zoo. We attended the annual pantomime at the Palace Theatre.

With Mum, Dad took great care of us boys.

In October 1953, Dad bought me a canary, 'Chippy', as my birthday present (15 shillings, 75p), and a light blue cage (£1 14s 6d, £1.73p). On his way back from work Dad would pick one or two pieces of groundsel for Chippy, bringing it home in the small brown case in which he carried his yellow and green sandwich tin, the book that he was reading at the time, and his torch. Then, when he ate an apple, Dad used to cut a slice and wedge it between the thin wire 'bars' of the cage, together with a piece of cuttlefish. I can see Dad doing it now, as gently as he could, with the occasional jerky, sudden movements of the arms that he was already developing. Mum told me that Dad used to hold Chippy carefully in his left hand and clip his nails with nail scissors. When Dad

became really ill, at the end of our second canary's life, the little
bird's nails grew long. Dad's hands were no longer steady enough to do
that job.

In December that year Dad bought Ralf and me a 'crown' (a five-
shilling piece) struck by the Royal Mint to commemorate the Coronation. Ralf and I awaited the arrival of this present with great
excitement.

As spring arrived in February 1954, Dad bought a Conference pear
tree, which bore beautiful and lavish fruit until Mum's death forty-four
years later, when it too died. The tree cost 17s 11d (just under 90p), and
it came from Chalice's nursery in Plympton, where Mum's brother
Arthur had worked when he and his wife Edna were setting up their
floristry business in the 1930s.

In March, Dad bought me a black Parker fountain pen, like his own,
in preparation for my transfer to a new school in September. It saw me
through Oxford and Cambridge.

After our holiday at the caravan in August, Dad's old friend Tony
Lawrance, the padre in Saugor, visited us. With his second wife, Myrtle,
he brought us a puppy, our first family dog. 'Patch' was a mongrel, half
English bull-terrier, from the litter that the Lawrances had bred at
Walkington, the village between Beverley and Hull in Yorkshire to which
Tony had moved as Rector, after his years at Barmston.

In the same month Dad and Mum took me to Dingle's department
store in Plymouth. They spent £33 (a fortune for them) to fit me out
with what I needed for my first term at the preparatory school for
Plymouth College.

For an eight-year-old, there was something exciting and curiously
grown up about the smell of the uniforms in the schools department –
sturdy wooden cabinets, displaying all the little blazers and short
trousers, the rugby kit and gaberdine raincoats. In quiet groups, parents
were gathered with their children, preparing for the autumn term and
its games of rugby on the lush, green playing fields, marked out with
sharp chalk lines.

In those weeks, Dad paid Mr Foale £30 to redecorate the hall, landing
and staircase, which transformed the house for us. Unusually, that
month's expenditure exceeded income by £30, and it did the same in
September by £14. From time to time Dad was still lending or giving
money to members of Mum's family (£1 in December, for example, to
Hilda and Fred).

Soon after I started to attend the prep school in September, Dad had a short posting to Bridgwater. It may have been devoted to further weapons training, needed to secure Coypool during the IRA's campaign of terrorism.

During his time at Bridgwater Dad went up to London to visit Mum's Uncle Jack and Aunt Alice in London. Nellie had died and Jack had remarried. Like Uncle Jack, and Aunt Nellie before her, Alice took to Dad. The three of them attended the theatre in the West End, and Dad brought back some piano music for Mum, including *Getting to Know You*, from *The King and I*. Mum often played and sang this song.

This was Dad's last independent travel away from home. It was at home that he found his confidence with Mum and, I hope, with us boys. Later, in his early weeks at Moorhaven Hospital, he sometimes said, *'Take me back to no.10, Moorland Road, please.'*

At Christmas, Dad and Mum gave me my first bicycle (£15 5s 6d, £15.27), green with three gears; and Ralf inherited my blue tricycle.

It had been an expensive year, but Dad knew what he was doing. In January 1955 he received a back-dated pay rise. As Mum often told me later, Dad came in one morning from night duty and, sitting on the edge of their bed, opened the fat pay packet, with £39 back-pay. Evidently I fully shared their pleasure at this: Dad let me write, quite neatly, *'Ha Ha! Ha Ha!'* in his account book alongside that entry.

We all celebrated by attending *Cinderella* just after Christmas (*'good,'* Dad let me write in his notebook). The next day was Ralf's birthday, for which he received a clockwork train set (£1 15s 0d, £1.75p). Hilda and Fred received another loan or gift of £1.

❦

As the years had slipped by, Kathleen visited us less often on Sunday afternoons and then her visits stopped completely. Perhaps Dad and Mum had noticed that Kathleen's chorea was somehow unsettling me; Ralf was probably still too young to take it in.

Instead of staying in for Kathleen, we started to go to Hilda's for Sunday afternoon tea. Dad did not often come on those visits to Hilda. I now realise that he used to stay at home so that Kathleen could call on him at no.10 to take her bath and spend some time with him there. Sometimes he visited her at her lodgings.

Kathleen became so unwell that she had to be admitted as a patient at Moorhaven Hospital for the rest of her life. Mum felt guilty about this. She so much wished to help her, but there was nothing she could do. Kathleen's condition, and its still faint and hazy reflection in Dad, must have been difficult to bear.

Dad was devoted to Kathleen. He often visited her at the hospital on his day off. What he saw happening to her must, in itself, have affected him deeply. There were also the fears for Mum and his sons, as well as for his own health.

In 1962 Dad arranged for a simple, beautiful grave for Kathleen, made of red granite. The inscription on the headstone in St Mary's church-yard reads: *'In God's keeping.'*

She was forty-nine years old.

Quite soon after the New Year in 1955, when we went to *Cinderella*, I seem to have begun to sense more strongly – I was now well into in my tenth year – what was happening to Dad. Mrs Gardiner, at the infants' school, had told Mum that I absorbed things like blotting-paper. It was at the same age that my cousin Barbara took in what was going on in the case of her mother Clara.

At the end of the winter, in March 1955, Ralf caught mumps at the primary school, and I caught it from him. Ralf quickly recovered, but I developed unexplained 'complications'. As a result, I missed the whole of my first summer term at the preparatory school and then stayed down to repeat that year. The medical notes report that I was anxious because I had heard Dr Owen say that, if Dad caught mumps, *'It could be serious for him at his age.'* My anxiety must have been severe, for Dr Owen prescribed phenol-barbitone, and a consultant paediatrician visited no. 10 to examine me. The consultation cost four guineas.

During those four months at home, often in bed, I studied Dad's two Hindustani text books and became quite fluent, writing in the cursive Urdu script that Dad used. I kept a diary in the script. It is a sign of my closeness at that time to Dad and his interests. He kindled my love of languages. It was surely my growing sense of the changes taking place in him that caused this jolt in my health.

Somehow the penny had dropped. Dad was changing, becoming less himself, less capable, less than the full person whom, as a tiny boy, I had known and still now loved so much; becoming more like poor Auntie Kath.

So I suffered a crisis, and, as Barbara explained, I began gradually to withdraw from him, just to protect myself from the unexplained, frightening changes.

My withdrawal must have been at least as painful for Dad at the time as it remains for me as I recall it now. *'How much he loved you boys!'* Mum used to say to me.

It is a pain that will not go away. It has also been a means of staying close to him over the years.

In writing this book about him and his family, I have grown so close to him that it is as if I now know him as he was when he flourished.

PART THREE

19
Interlude

THIS IS DAD'S story, and part of Mum's, but the constant presence of this dread, this sense of being at risk from something you cannot change, is so difficult to understand that I will try to explain it from my own experience.

One Sunday afternoon in September 2002, I was driving on the A361 road between Devizes and its junction with the A4, near Avebury and Silbury Hill. It was a beautiful autumn day, with the golden sun lying quite low over the fields that stretch northeast to the Marlborough downs.

Something was familiar, but not immediately obvious. After a while, I realised what it was. I thought: *'This is the road I used to travel with Ralf on our way back to Oxford at the end of each vacation between 1966 and 1968.'* I used to pull the Morris Minor (PCO 293) into a lay-by where the road ran past the edge of a copse of alder trees beside a little lake, and there we would eat the Cornish pasties that Mum had cooked for us for the journey. Not many cars would pass us while we ate. The road was quiet in those days.

And for the next few minutes, as I remembered all this, in a deep silence, I experienced again what it used to be, to live without the risk of Huntington's.

The stillness and the empty road and the steady motion of the car and the recollection of that lay-by with its alder trees and the view across the open country to the Downs, which I had not seen for nearly thirty-four years, cast a spell on me. I was free.

The spell held me and comforted me as long as I was on that road. It was broken as soon as I turned onto the A4, on which I have driven once or twice since I learnt from Dr Owen that I was at risk on the twenty-sixth day of February 1969.

This is the only time in the years since those days that this sensation of freedom, of all the generosity of life and its possibilities has flooded into my consciousness.

And so I learnt afresh from those few minutes the pattern of what Dad and Mum went through.

From sometime in 1950 they knew that something terrible was afoot. And the knowledge that it was happening could never wholly leave them, yet they did everything for us. That is the measure of their courage and faithfulness.

They bore the knowledge and dread on our behalf as long as they could. They did us a great good.

It was good to live knowing nothing of that risk.

20

The Two of Them, Together

DAD SAVED the situation when I was ill for so many weeks in the summer of 1955.

He rented the caravan at Challaborough for an extra fortnight in June. There was hardly anyone else there, so early in the season. We had the beach to ourselves. The weather was wonderful.

On our Vidor radio, we listened to Max Robertson's exciting commentaries on the tennis championships at Wimbledon. We were cheering on Jaroslav Drobny who had won the men's singles championship the previous year when he was already well over thirty years old, but in 1955 he lost in the first round. It was not his success in 1954 but his mysterious name and nationality (a Yugoslav, exiled to Egypt), and his age, that put us on his side. We played our version of tennis, as well as cricket, on the grass beside the caravan, and enjoyed the sea air and swimming.

Dad's plan worked. The time at the caravan in June, and the usual two weeks in August, for which Dad paid Mr Pascoe £10 altogether, revived us all. I recovered my health.

In August he and Mum had a modern fireplace installed in the sitting-room, and in December Dad bought an Ekco television set with a seventeen-inch screen.

$$\mathbb{Q}$$

From time to time, in the 1950s, I gained an inkling of how his commission in the Army had changed Dad's life. In those days BBC television used, each autumn, to show the Prime Minister's speech at the annual banquet of the incoming Lord Mayor of London. One evening

Dad and I were in the sitting-room, by the coal fire, watching the grand scene in Guildhall, with all the guests in evening dress, at long tables elegantly laid with silver and glass. Dad was sitting with his legs crossed on the carpet, as he often did when we were on our own at home in the family, a throw-back, I liked to think, to life in the jungle. *'Soup – fish – joint – pudding – savoury,'* Dad said, and repeated it for me, with a smile, recalling the monthly formal dinners that he enjoyed in the officers' mess for those few years. And he explained to me about savouries, such as 'devils-on-horseback', of which I had never heard.

It is a lovely evening, a time for just the two of us; Mum is helping Ralf to get ready for bed: just the two of us on our own, Dad and me, just how I like it. But as I sit there on the sofa and Dad is squatting on the hearthrug, I must be taking in the way in which he is changing; taking it in without allowing myself to acknowledge it.

It may be the same experience as Dad had as a boy when his grandfather John Hocking and his Uncle Frank began to be affected by Huntington's.

Gradually the changes in Dad seep into my mind, so surreptitiously that I am not conscious of noticing them or identifying them for what they are. I just experience the external effects of what is happening deep within every cell of Dad's body. I slowly begin to take it for granted that Dad's movements are not exactly like those of everyone else, except of course for Auntie Kathleen's. A few years earlier I had seen the same thing in her when she used to visit us every Sunday afternoon, but by this time she is a patient at Moorhaven Hospital and is much further on the road to Calvary.

So Dad squats on his haunches, and every so often, unexpectedly, he shrugs his shoulders or brings his knees together; he opens his eyes rather wider than usual and then relaxes them; his fingers twitch a little or come to rest at slightly unusual angles; his head occasionally lolls back a little before correcting itself. But all this is so slight, so sneaky that I do not realise what is happening.

Yet, unconsciously, I *am* taking it all in. And it is happening, and the disease is changing Dad's consciousness, his state of mind. He and I are already slipping apart, he and Mum, and he and Ralf, he and the rest of the world – not that I care about the rest of the world, – it's *us*, the four of us, whom I want to scream and weep and rage about: it's *we three* who love him, whom he loves (of course, in my *head* I know that all the others matter so much, too). So he and I are slipping apart, and in this life there can be no retrieval, no going back. And this unexplained slipping apart will lead to terrible mistakes on my part and unbearable sadness that can never end – not in this life, it can't.

So all this is happening, unknown to me, as Dad and I sit watching the Prime Minister, Mr Macmillan, speak in Guildhall, lamenting with his charming, lugubrious, effortless irony, which gives such comfort, that his job does not give him time to watch *The Lone Ranger* on Saturday afternoons. Whatever else we face, at least Dad and I, and Mum and Ralf, can do that together sometimes.

❧

At school I began to forge ahead. But my growing devotion to study was to become my way of distancing myself from what was happening to Dad, an escape from the inexplicable pain surrounding us all, more sharply year by year. The only way out that I found was, I suppose, to become the centre of my own universe. I protected myself by closing my eyes, shutting my ears. The gradual loss of the one who had given so much joy steadily constricted me and contracted my life, as if it were throttling me. I could not breathe normally.

Our strong family life, the pattern that Dad and Mum had built, saved us because soon after this Dad's strength began to ebb more noticeably. The pattern was set – a good pattern, a steady, well-balanced pattern for our life together, but Dad's energy and initiative waned, slowly, so slowly.

You can see it in his handwriting in the last in the series of his little account books, begun in May 1952. By 1955 and 1956 his hand has become less tidy and graceful, contrasting distressingly with the neat, small script of earlier days and previous notebooks.

And then there is an undated entry, probably coming from some time between late 1954 and early 1956. It reads '£60-13s-2d Dr. Blu'. It was apparently replaced by an even larger sum, £98 14s 0d.

'Dr. Blu' seems to be an abbreviation. It seems almost certain that, in one way or another, there was a series of consultations with an extremely expensive specialist doctor. It is possible that Dad consulted him, clearly more than once, in Harley Street when he visited London and stayed with Uncle Jack and Aunt Alice in October 1954, during his training course at Bridgwater.

Dad also wrote in a small address book, in capital letters, the word *'FENTAZINE'*, a drug used at that time to diminish the delusions and other psychotic symptoms of Huntington's patients. Perhaps this refers to medication prescribed for Auntie Kath, and perhaps she and Auntie Clara went with Dad, or separately, to consult *Dr. Blu*. That might explain the size of the fees, and Dad would probably have paid their travelling expenses.

Whatever the details of these consultations, the certainty is that Dad's condition was now worsening. It is likely that he felt the need for the best information and advice from an expert, and there were few experts in Huntington's in those days. Perhaps he and Mum had been able to hope against hope until then for some sort of release from what was happening, but at some time between late 1954 and early 1956 that hope died.

By now, more members of Mum's family were noticing what was happening to Dad's health.

Mum's brother Wally noticed a pale reflection in Dad of Kathleen's much more advanced symptoms. Since we had moved to Plympton in 1950, we had seen quite a lot of his family. Wally's son Richard remembers that when he was seventeen years old, his father had told him that he thought that Dad was developing the same illness as Kathleen. He can date this accurately to a little before or a little after July 1955, when he left school. At around the same time, Richard was also told by his father, or Richard overheard him say, that Dad had 'gone to west Cornwall' to consult the doctors and medical records about Kathleen and Clara's deteriorating condition. Richard himself has no clear recollection of a time when Dad was really fit and well.

Others saw what was happening, especially the shopkeepers in Ridgeway in Plympton. It was a quiet high street in those days, as well as the main road (the A 38) between Plymouth and Exeter. Plympton was still a village of about six thousand souls, and most people did almost all their weekly shopping in Ridgeway. The shopkeepers were 'fixtures', staying for many years; they were our friends.

Mrs Pearce, the owner of the hardware shop, and Mum were good friends. In the mid-1950s she noticed that Dad was getting ill. *'He was always so nice to talk to – a gentleman. It was very sad to see him going like that, very sad. I first noticed it when I was speaking to him. He began to shake a bit. It began to affect his speaking; it made his voice falter. It was dreadful that he was ill for so long – dreadful.'*

Susan Pearce, her eldest daughter and one year younger than me, also noticed it in the mid-1950s. She cannot remember a time when Dad was really well. Especially, she recalls Dad's uneven, unsteady walk, and that Mum *'was always there for him, holding his arm, steadying him if he lost his balance'.*

That is how I remember it. They faced it, the two of them, together. Mr Kelly at the grocery shop saw it too. In the early 1950s he was a commercial traveller for a wholesale grocer and he used to visit several shops in Ridgeway. At some time in those years, he noticed Dad's strange walk. *'You couldn't* help *noticing it,'* he told me, almost as if, out of his affection for Dad, he wished that it had been possible not to see what was happening, and to see only the true heart of Dad. Mr Kelly had noticed his unsteady movements well before 1958, the year when he began to work full-time at Mr Rhodes' shop. He later bought the shop, and he and his wife ran it until 1980. Mum and Dad did much of their shopping there, and the four of them became good friends. Mr Kelly told me:

'You could tell that he was intelligent. But now he was limited in what he could do. It was as if he couldn't manage any longer to use all his intelligence. His speech was a bit slurred and his vocabulary was a little limited, but he had all his faculties. We used to talk about everyday things.

He kept his mind focused on what he was doing at the moment. He used to have a list from Mrs. Symons of what he had to buy. His walk was uneven, with some long strides, then short ones, as if he were avoiding the cracks in the pavement, and then he would sometimes hesitate before walking on. He was always on the move and sometimes staggered. We knew, of course, that he hardly drank anything, but his gait made him look drunk. It was his walk that I noticed first.

He was a gentleman, such a nice person, and it was such a sad ending after his career. He was kindness itself, and people respected him. It was very sad – they were both such nice people.'

Mr Kelly added:

'It was as if he was sorry to be inflicting the condition he was in on the people he met. Your Mum was a gem for him. She helped him keep occupied. They were a devoted couple.

Your Dad took to Mrs. Kelly and me and we used to talk. We were good friends. He had a lot of knowledge and he was interesting to talk to. Then he would lapse into silence and go on his way.'

Mr Kelly remembered, too, how sympathetic our neighbours at no. 8 (Walter and Nancy Pearse) were about Dad's affliction when they visited him to do their shopping. The Pearses once told me that they felt that, because of what happened to Dad, they had never known him.

'*I remember your* mother', one neighbour from those years said to me, but her tone of voice changed immediately when I asked about Dad. '*It was nearly fifty years ago,*' Mrs Gray said. How could I blame her? She, too, averted her eyes from what was happening. Yet, for many years Dad gave regularly to the British and Foreign Bible Society, for which Mrs Gray's husband, a clergyman, worked in Plympton, from 1953 to 1956.

Mary Davis, another neighbour, took in more of what was happening. Mary lived around the corner from us, in one of the comfortable, detached houses built in the 1950s, whose red brick Mum admired so much. Mary became one of Mum's dearest friends in later years. She told me:

'*Unfortunately, I never really came across your father. I don't recall ever talking to him. Your mother and I would talk at your front garden gate, and I got the impression that he was sitting in the kitchen. When Andrew [Mary's son] went through the house to play with you in the back garden, he told me that he saw your father sitting there – he was 'tall and quiet and nice', Andy told me.*

I never really saw him or had the chance to have a talk with him. At first I just assumed that he was very quiet and retiring, but as time passed I felt that it must be something to do with his health. I just felt that something strange was happening.'

This invisibility to others, this non-existence that overtakes those with Huntington's, adds another sort of sadness to those who love its victims.

Those years were unusually wet in South Devon, even by its lavish standards of rain. By now Dad had for some time been taking the number 21 bus to work. Joe and his wife, Jessie, lived in one of the terrace of houses by the bus stop at Coypool. Jessie and Joe invited Dad to stand in the porch of their house to wait for the bus when it was raining. Their son, Alan, remembers Dad waiting there. He first noticed the signs of Dad's illness soon after his own father's tragic death from cancer, in middle age, in May 1957. Alan was then in his early teens.

Everyone in Plympton trusted Jessie as the wise, kind, discreet and brilliantly efficient secretary and receptionist at Dr Owen's surgery. With Miss Doris Knight, the pharmacist at Kirkness, the chemist in Ridgeway, she saved the doctors in the practice many wasted hours and the two of them resolved many problems.

Of course, Jessie knew what was happening, and it was to her that I went on the morning in February 1969 when I learnt the meaning of Dad's illness. In addition to everything else, Jessie had a fierce loyalty and a wonderful sense of humour. After being awarded his outstanding degree at Oxford University, Alan entered the examination for a prize fellowship at All Souls College. That year, the son of the Bishop of Exeter was elected. Jessie commented to Mum, *'If Joe had been a bloody bishop, Alan would have been a fellow of All Souls!'*

So, through the 1950s, this perception that something terrible was happening to Dad spread from the family to friends and acquaintances.

I lived too close to it all to take it in. I explained everything away in order to make the strangeness of it all bearable, to keep my balance. I was lucky to have those years of not knowing, but I am not proud of the way that I allowed the barrier, which I built in order to shield myself from the sadness, to affect my behaviour. Others suffered from that. At the time perhaps I could not have had the one without the other, and I had to try to keep myself safe.

I had no idea of what was happening, and I am glad.

21

No Way Out

DAD WAS NOW in the second half of his fifties, and some sort of crisis was smouldering, for him and for all four of us. He was gradually slipping into the background of my life. I shut my eyes and directed my mind elsewhere, but, however hard you try, you cannot completely close your heart or deaden your senses.

Only once more was there a big event – important for me, that is, – which Dad decisively affected. In the summer term of 1959, he visited 'HD' (Hugh Dent), my form master at the College, and discussed with him whether I should begin to study German or ancient Greek when I moved up to the third form in September.

By now it must have been a great test for Dad to do this for me. There was always something painful and poignant in the way Mum, in later years, emphasised to me how much Mr Dent had liked and respected Dad, as if to reassure me. After that meeting, 'HD' seemed to adopt an especially kind and thoughtful attitude towards me. It was as if he were now aware of some unusual need in me: as if he had solved some puzzle that he had been turning over in his mind ever since he began to teach me a year or so earlier. The decision that he and Dad took together was in favour of Greek, and it proved a good decision.

For his Christmas present that year Dad bought me a stainless steel wristwatch from J. W. Benson of Bond Street. I am wearing it now; it keeps true time. It was from Benson's that Dad had bought his half-hunter watch when he and Mum were on honeymoon.

The months passed. I slaved at my books. Dad and Mum gave me gentle encouragement and support.

Of course, I now know that many parents will do almost anything for their children, going the extra mile, turning the other cheek, giving them the clothing from their back, going out to meet the returning Prodigal. Yet there is something heart-rending in the way Dad, and along with him Mum, yielded up everything for us. Dad's internal resources were diminishing, and at an accelerating rate. Time was against all four of us, but they saw through to the end faithfully and successfully what they had begun.

Just occasionally something of what was happening to Dad got through my blinkers.

One sunny Saturday afternoon in 1958 or 1959 Uncle George (Mum's brother) called on us. It had never happened before. It meant something. Even at the time I could sense that. I felt frightened.

Uncle George was wearing his best three-piece dark suit. He still made his living from the fruit-and-vegetable stall in the covered market in Plymouth, which Uncle Arthur had arranged for him in the 1930s. In this way, Arthur had managed to rescue his brother from working at the china clay works at Lee Moor, which was damaging his health.

Uncle Arthur's plan to give George a steady job and a reliable way of earning his living had worked out, although there was the occasional crisis caused by George's gambling and intermittent drinking, combined with his over-generosity when he won 'on the horses'. Once, as Uncle Arthur slipped him half a crown to bale him out of some debt in the 1930s, he said, *'Here it is, waster.'* On Saturdays George usually shared the stall with Hilda, and together they did a good trade.

Dad's account book shows that, from time to time, he lent or gave George small sums of money to help him out, but by that day in 1958 or 1959 it was no longer possible or perhaps wise for him to do so. Dad was already hard pressed by his illness and his care for us. Now he had to summon up the resources to refuse George his request for a loan, much bigger than in the past. Probably George's younger brother Wally had already refused him.

Dad and George discussed this on good terms, and George left cheerfully enough, but I find it difficult to comprehend or, in my heart, even now to forgive his shade for what he put Dad through. But then I remember how many people forgave George so much because of his frank and open nature. In the nursing home where his life drew to its end, Mum visited him faithfully, and she saw how the nurses and other staff warmed to him because of his kindliness and generous spirit.

George knew himself and his faults. When his father offered him, then a little boy of about five years, and his brothers and sisters a sprig of honeysuckle plucked from high in the hedge in Stuggy Lane, George had said *'Give it to me, Daddy – I's the g'eedy boy.'*

Perhaps I also feel that Mum should have told her brother that his behaviour was unacceptable, but probably it had to come from Dad, even if Mum had an inkling of what to expect from George (and she may not have). Somehow George found the money to get by. He always did.

This incident had a big impact on me at the time, although Dad and Mum never mentioned it again in my hearing. It was the cost which, even then, I felt that it exacted from Dad that made it so painful; and the sense it gave me that our life was so fragile.

Ten or eleven years earlier, at Venton, it had been Dad who gave me his hand to hold and steadied me as we walked together up the lane from the well to Saugor Cottage. The comforting grip that had kept me safe was now unsure and weakening, and Dad and I could do nothing about it.

A year later, during the summer holidays, I came in from a cycle ride. I remember going to the front bedrooms upstairs to look at the sunset. Dad was lying on the bed, listening to the Henry Wood promenade concert on the radio. In a flash I saw that he had an inner life of his own, a love of music, a need for peace and quiet and restoration. For some reason, I had a hollow sense within me, a fearful, inexplicable feeling that he was slipping away to a distance that could not be bridged.

ℚ

In the late 1950s and early 1960s we usually had four weeks' holiday at the caravan. Dad would be with us for two or three weeks; then he would return home to work at Coypool.

On his days off he used to travel out by bus to Bigbury-on-Sea to stay with us. We would walk over the cliffs from Challaborough to meet him at the bus stop. Sometimes I went there in the evening to meet him on my own. Dad and I would walk back to the caravan, cosy and warm, lighted softly by its Calor gas lamps. Mum would make us cocoa when we arrived.

That walk with Dad used to make me happy, in the old way. The beam of light from our chrome-plated torch would pick out moths rising from the tall tufts of grass along the sandy footpath, and Dad and I would talk, and I would experience his care and concern for me, his interest in what I was doing and learning. He was quiet and withdrawn by now, but, on our own like that, I suppose I felt as I had when we were walking up the hill at Venton together. Even on holiday I studied endlessly, as an escape from what was happening. Those walks together were a release from the need to escape. Through being alone with him, concentrating just on him, with nothing to distract either of us, and in the dusk I found peace; we found peace together. As Dad's capacities weakened, Mum's instinct was to seek to fill the gap, the silences. It was rare that Dad and I were alone together and I was able really to be in touch with him.

They both did the best they could, but Huntington's had the whip-hand over us all.

In 1960 I bought a colour film for my Kodak box camera, of which I was very proud. In one photograph, taken by Ralf, Mum and I are shown together on the cliff path to Bigbury, accompanying Dad to catch the bus back to work after a couple of days with us. In Dad's face, I see the worry and the anxiety of the situation; in Mum's, the urgency to smile and to make things as well as they could be. My face is a mask.

℺

One night, late in the autumn of 1961 or during the early months of 1962, I awoke with a start. There was a brief clattering sound and some muffled words.

Tired by the routine of the daily journeys to and from school in Plymouth and by all my study, I sank back into sleep. Ralf did the same.

Outside our bedrooms on the landing, Dad had mistaken his direction and stumbled on his way back to bed from the lavatory. He had fallen down the stairs – all eighteen of them. It may have been a sign that his Huntington's was on the move. It was a decisive moment, and after the fall Dad's health deteriorated more quickly.

Cousin Barbara visited us at this time, soon after her marriage. She noticed Dad's condition with alarm.

For the first time in ten years Mum was ill, with varicose ulcers, brought on, I am sure, by what was happening to Dad. Apart from our caravan holidays (we all felt safe there), there were no more outings or activities for us as a family.

Just before we went to Challaborough in July 1962, Dad made his Will.

℺

It must have taken a great effort on my part to blind myself, to convince myself that what was happening to Dad, to all of us, was not out of the ordinary, but somehow I managed to do so. It was vital to succeed in this, to protect myself and my education.

Unconsciously, I must have seen that as the only way to escape from what I was experiencing – the gradual, ineluctable removal of the one who, with Mum, but more than her, had made me safe and protected me. From what he did and said, from his character, from his care and gentleness to me, from how I felt about him deep within me, I knew him to be completely true and reliable. Yet the gap caused by Huntington's between us was widening all the time. Other people could not see him for what I knew he was and had done, for his true worth, and this was more than I could bear.

There could be no escape.

We all did our best.

Stranger on the Shore:
Challaborough beach, 1952-1963
(St John's Gospel, Ch 21, v 1-14)

He stands there, hidden in the mist,
And holds the towels;
Blue eyes and silver hair,
Soft shirt and cardigan.

And on another shore, beside another sea,
Tiberias, there stands
Another Man, who makes a fire and cooks
The fish for breakfast.

And in the mist they merge
And, without the one,
The other loses all significance.
Before Christ was my Father is.

22

'I love you, my darling'

DAD RETIRED at the end of March 1963.

It had been the hardest winter since 1947. Spring came late that year. Even in Devonshire the ground was hard with frost until the equinox.

The commanding officer at Coypool wrote Dad a farewell letter, thanking him for his loyal, good work for twelve years. He mentioned, with special gratitude, that Dad made his way to work every day, and night, that winter, often walking the two miles there and the two miles back through the snow.

Dad's colleagues were sorry to lose him. They visited him at home at no. 10 one afternoon and presented him with a Parker fountain pen which had a stainless steel case. It was a modern version of the one that he had used for so long.

With Mum's support and guidance, Dad established a new routine. Each morning, he would take the wicker shopping-basket (I have it still) and, carrying it over the crook of his left arm, go to Ridgeway to do the shopping, with a list prepared by Mum.

Usually he went first to Mr and Mrs Kelly's grocery shop. Then he would cross the road to visit Mr Vibert at the butcher's shop, and pass Mrs Hawkins' ladies' outfitters where Mum bought her clothes. He would collect the newspaper at Muldowney's stationery shop.

These outings each morning, on his own, were important for Dad. Although some of the shopkeepers sometimes worried that, without Mum's steadying arm, he might fall over, that happened only once or twice in all those years, towards the end when his choreic movements were much more sudden and jerky.

128

Mum knew how important it was for Dad to go out alone and do this shopping. Once, for a moment revealing their sadness (it hardly ever happened), she told me how much it hurt Dad that *'he could do so little'*.

At home, Dad would bring in the coal for the fire in the sitting-room and for the Rayburn, and he would do the dusting. I see him now dusting the stairs, kneeling on each of them as he worked his way down to the hall. He was able to continue to cut the grass for a while.

Mum and Dad took me to Dingle's department store to fit me out to go to Oxford. They bought a wonderful aluminium-lined trunk, two sports jackets (this was 1964, when students still wore 'real' clothes), two pairs of trousers, a tea-set, tea towels, a dressing-gown (I still wear it sometimes) and a small portable radio (an Ekco, like our television set). How did they afford it? I had worked as a deliveryman for the South Western Electricity Board after I left school, but my wages did not pay for all these treasures.

Then came a beautiful September, and we basked in the sun. It was the sunniest and driest September in Devonshire that century.

And then I was gone. The train pulled slowly up Hemerdon bank, the steepest stretch of mainline track on the old Great Western Railway. I passed the wood known as 'the Plantation', where Dad and Mum waved to me, and looked out at Stuggy Lane where, so often, we had walked together, the four of us.

℞

Ralf became lonely. Mum and Dad bought him a golden Labrador, 'Rusty', as red as his name. He became their companion on their daily walks. They had a long walk every day.

After Dad had done his shopping, he and Mum would set out with Rusty up the long hill that rises gently to the east, the continuation of Ridgeway, as far as the drive of Chaddlewood House. In those years there were open fields and a herd of dairy cows. The house is now surrounded by an immense, forlorn housing estate, a dormitory for Plymouth, built in the late 1970s and 1980s.

On other days, they would walk northwards, beyond Torridge and the 'Plantation' and under the railway bridge to Newnham House.

Then, on their return, they would sit down at the pine table in the kitchen for the stew that they had left cooking slowly in the Rayburn. We called it 'peasant food'. Later, they would enjoy afternoon tea by the fire in the sitting-room.

On Sundays, there was church, St Mary's, where they had been married. Because of his choreic movements, Dad was embarrassed about receiving the Holy Communion. For this reason he had ceased attending the early 8 o'clock service by the mid-1950s. So their service was Evensong. In the university vacation we sometimes joined them in their pew, half-hidden beside one of the granite columns in the north aisle.

Who can tell, but I have the strong impression that this routine supported them, and for several years gave them the strength and peace and contentment that they needed to keep things going. This sense of Dad and Mum's steady, peaceful routine also saved me. I owe everything to them.

Two years later Ralf joined me at Oxford.

Our parents' routine became less easy as Dad's condition worsened. In the spring of the year that Ralf joined me at Oxford, 1966, I cancelled a trip to Greece to visit the archaeological sites because of my anxiety about Dad. A year later I received a travel scholarship from my College. I hesitated. My ancient history tutor asked me, not unkindly but in ignorance, *'Can't someone else look after your parents while you are away?'* I doubted it and did not know how to reply, but with two friends from the College I made the trip and spent five weeks there. The classics came more alive for me than ever.

On my return from Greece, Dad's condition shocked me. It seemed so much worse, but I had to return with Ralf to Oxford a few days later.

There was a crisis soon after we left no. 10. Mum had to make a visit to the doctor's surgery. Dr Owen's note records that she was suffering from anxiety and loss of appetite. He also wrote, *'her husband is in hospital'*. Of this Mum and Dad told us nothing.

By the time we returned to no. 10 in June for the long vacation, their old routine had been restored and Dad's short stay in Moorhaven Hospital seemed to have stabilised the situation.

That summer we had many happy afternoons together, with picnics by a remote stream at a place that we called Lane End, on the edge of Dartmoor, just as we had done in 1966. We were able to do the same in 1968 after I took my degree. My car made this possible. It was a Morris Minor 1000, PCO 293. I had bought it in April 1966 when I finished the first part of my degree. For the purpose I used the expired National Savings Certificates that Dad had bought for me many years earlier. It was a strange use to make of his hard-earned money, and in many circumstances it would have been foolish. Yet that hasty decision proved to be one of the best I ever made. That Morris gave us pure joy at a time when we needed it.

@

In October I went to Cambridge to read for a further degree. The following Christmas was not easy for any of us. Then, in late February 1969, I came home again for a few days.

Immediately, I realised that the game was up. The pressure on Mum was unbearable.

In the middle of one night, when I got up to go to the lavatory, the light was burning on the landing. There was a note in Mum's handwriting lying on the rug just outside my door. It was written in biro on a piece of cardboard from a skein of the wool that Mum used for darning our socks. The note said (I still have it), *'John, we leave the light on overnight on the landing,'* a safety precaution for Dad and their peace of mind.

The next day, the twenty-sixth, I called on Dr Owen to talk to him about the situation. In his dry way, he expressed his concern. I asked him if the condition was 'congenital'. *'I'm sorry to have to tell you that it is hereditary,'* he said.

I stumbled out of the surgery and walked to Marsh Mills and called on Jessie, Mum and Dad's old friend. Jessie gave me a cup of coffee. She told me that she knew of Dad's affliction. *'Is it Huntington's chorea?'* she said. We talked. She was very kind.

Afterwards, I walked up the old railway track to Plymbridge. In my confusion, I knew that my life was changed at a stroke. I walked home.

Later that day I told Mum, in the kitchen, that Dr Owen had explained the situation to me. Mum looked worried. We agreed that, as soon as his exams were safely written in June, she should tell Ralf about it. She did so, the most terrible thing imaginable for her. Ralf had been able to take his exams in reasonable peace of mind. That mattered.

By the skin of our teeth, we made it.

Back in Cambridge, I decided to terminate my course. I applied for jobs and joined the Civil Service. I started work in the Treasury in October. I was determined to earn my living and, if possible, to make some contribution to my parents.

It worked out.

In August that year, while I was still in Cambridge and was applying for jobs, Dad had to be admitted to Moorhaven as a permanent patient.

He was able to return home to no.10 only once, for Christmas the following year. My friend Susan's sister, Margaret, lent me her mini van, and I was able to collect and return Dad safely. It was a beautiful day, frosty and sunny. We all enjoyed it.

For three years Dad lived as a patient at the hospital. The staff liked him; they respected him. They saw something of what he was. Mum visited him three times a week, travelling on the special bus from Plymouth to the hospital at Bittaford, twelve miles east of Plympton. Often she visited him every day. Somehow, she found time to bake buns for him, sometimes enough for all the patients in his ward. When I was able to get down from London I used to hire a car and take Dad and Mum for a drive. We used to go to Lane End, with its many happy memories.

As Dad settled in at the hospital, he became more stable. His weight went up to 9st 6lb, and his face filled out and had a good colour. He used to help Mum do the *Daily Telegraph* cryptic crossword. Once she wrote to me, *'I was doing the crossword on Wednesday and didn't know how to spell "trigonometry", and Dad knew! I asked him and he spelt it immediately. I was so pleased. His brain is very active.'*

In March 1971 Judy and I got engaged. Mum wrote to me, *'I gently explained to Dad about you and Judy, and he seemed pleased, and agreed that it would be lovely for you to be happily married. I wish with all my heart that he were well enough to see the wedding; still, we have to be thankful that he is content, warm and comfortable. The nurse told me that they all think a great deal of him as he is so gentle.'*

Five months later Judy and I were married. She is very brave. It is her great regret that she never knew Dad.

Mum wrote to us as we settled into our first house, at Ely, *'It was a lovely, happy wedding and we all enjoyed it ... Judy looked beautiful, and you and Ralf handsome ... A day to remember.'*

She added, *'At the hospital, they told me that Dad was kicking a ball on the lawn while you and Judy were being married. Telepathy. We were happy and it was transported to him! I couldn't believe it, but the nice male nurse said it was so.'*

It happened just that once.

In the early months of 1972, a chest and stomach infection went around the ward three times. Mum told me, *'It has made Dad very poorly ... He sends his love. He always eats the egg custard that I bake for him, I'm glad to say.'*

In May Mum wrote to me, *'I go to the hospital every day as Dad is very poorly with this infection. Yesterday I took the colour snaps of Challaborough ... He seemed interested ... He is in bed until the infection clears up ... I go to Loughtor Mill every evening with Rusty and it tires me pleasantly for my night's rest.'*

Dad rallied a little, but became very thin. At the beginning of June Mum wrote, *'Dad had a temperature yesterday and I had to give him a lot to drink ... I now know what he means by "Help me", and I get the nurse to turn him. He is very thin, but the nurse said he is eating his meals and he drinks the milky coffee that I take him ... Sometimes I take a little bit of strawberry, caster sugar and cream, about four strawberries mashed up, and he eats this.'*

At the end of the month Mum told me, *'Dad is as comfortable as they can make him on the ripple bed, and the charge nurse says that he is such a good patient and never complains. The nurses are gentle and kind, and Dr Lilanwala is wonderful ... They are really doing all they can.'*

In mid-July, Dad developed a further chest infection, which turned to pneumonia. Ralf and I borrowed a friend's MG and raced down to the hospital from Cambridge.

That afternoon Dad said clearly to Mum, *'I love you, my darling,'* his last words.

Just before we arrived, as Mum was feeding him, Dad choked and lost his breath. It was a quick end. We kissed him on the forehead. He still had thick, white hair, neatly trimmed.

We drove down the steep lane, so like the hill at Venton where I have my first memory of Dad, and then made our way together, the three of us, home to no. 10.

They shall look on Him Whom they pierced
(St John's Gospel, Ch 19, v 37)

Those years are crumpled
and dishevelled
in my mind;

Like Dad then, dressing-
gown thrown open
and untied,

Pacing to and fro,
his hair uncombed,
gaunt eyes, wild;

With nothing cosy
left to comfort
or beguile

Him. How can I now
dissect the truth
which pierced us?

23

'Dearly loved husband, father and brother'

IT TOOK YEARS to take it all in.

It is difficult to remember the few months that followed Dad's death. Everything else is so clear in my memory. Once or twice, I believe, I went on the bus to Moorhaven Hospital. I wanted to recall how it had been in those last three years of Dad's life there.

In those three years the bus used to drop me at Bittaford, and I would slowly climb the hill, one-in-seven, or even one-in-five, under the railway viaduct. With me I would have the old brown plastic bucket-bag that I had used for so many years at the caravan, when I used to pack it with a towel and swimming trunks, and, later, with Homer's *Iliad* or *Odyssey* to read on the beach after a swim. When I had been visiting Dad in hospital, the bag had held a thermos of tea and two peaches. Peaches were soft, safe for me to peal and cut slices to give Dad, with no risk of his choking. His ability to swallow was affected by then.

I slip in through the heavy iron gates at the hospital lodge and walk up the long drive and through the grand, airy entrance hall. For the most part, the building is quiet, the atmosphere peaceful. The passages seem as long as the drive outside, and the rubbery linoleum deadens the sound as I walk. Wards open off the corridor every so often. Then, in the distance, I catch sight of Dad: a dark Cornish complexion, just over six feet tall, still with his slim build, but afflicted by a lurching, unsteady gait, shrugging his shoulders, eyes opening wider than is natural, head lolling a little to right or left from time to time.

Only in sleep is Dad at rest. Occasionally I see him like that, as I sit beside him in the ward.

Everyone in the ward likes Dad. They try to make things as nice as possible for him.

The notice of Dad's death that Mum had put in the newspaper testifies to this:

SYMONS: On July 22, after a long illness, including three years' devoted care at Moorhaven Hospital, Major William John Symons, MBE, IA (Retired), of Plympton, Devon, dearly beloved husband, father and brother. Funeral at Plympton St Mary's, two pm, July 26. Donations, if desired, to League of Friends of Moorhaven Hospital, Ivybridge, Devon.

❡

Another way that I tried to make sense of it all, in those days just after Dad died, was to go over the short talks we had been able to have, even in the last months at home. There was one that I often thought about. It would be easy to misunderstand it, yet in a way it expresses the most important thing about him. Without this, nothing makes sense. It is this that made it possible for him to live the life he lived.

Dad was wearing his dressing gown (I still have it), blue and grey, with a blue cord. It was the early summer of 1969, when Dad was as ill as it was possible to be without being admitted into care at Moorhaven. In those last months at home, he could not always get properly dressed – for all Mum's efforts, and his, to keep life as normal as possible for us.

So while Mum is shopping in Ridgeway, I am sitting with Dad in the dining-room. I try to divert him by reading him something from *The Forsyte Saga*, which he and Mum have recently watched on the television, but it does not help. Dad cannot concentrate; he cannot keep calm.

A few months ago Dad stopped reading. His glasses and the book, his last book, *Far From The Madding Crowd,* with a makeshift bookmark slipped in at the page where he stopped, are placed on the mantelpiece. This book and Dad's reading-glasses, in their worn, mottled, grey case, will stay there until we sell the house thirty one years later. One part of Dad's life died when he stopped reading. There were so many stations marking the way like that.

So, Dad is standing in the dining-room beside his old armchair. He is swaying a little, from side to side, to and fro; he lifts one leg or the other, and flexes his knees. He hunches up his shoulders and shrugs.

Then, for a moment, he is at rest and his mind is clear. He knows that he is with me; his voice is steady and calm. He looks me in the eye and says, *'Before this I trusted God completely.'* The moment of peace passes. It seemed that the world had stood still. Dad is all unwilled movement again.

Dad's words hit me in the heart and crush the breath out of me. My eyes sting and my spine tingles. I just sit there, gingerly on the edge of the second armchair, the one that Dad cannot use any more.

A few weeks ago his body and limb movements were so fierce that he was thrown sideways; he fell from the chair, and the force that was whipping through his body broke one of its back legs. I mended it in a rough and ready way, screwing it together. We cannot throw the chair away. Money is short now.

'Before this I trusted God completely.'

And I know that it is true. Dad is true, through and through.

But the question that hits me in a second wave, and makes my eyes sting again, is this. Was it all in vain?

This trust, this faith was growing in him from the first. It was handed down by his grandparents and his parents. And this faith, this attitude, is there already in Dad's hand as it rests lightly on his mother's left shoulder in the family photograph taken just after her husband's death. It is there, in the way the seven children regularly went to church and chapel, Sunday by Sunday. It is there, in the firm writing in the prayer- and hymn-book with which Dad was issued or which he bought in India: *'5430269 Pte. J. Symons. A/Coy 1/DCLI, Lucknow, India, 9 November 1924'*; in the Family Bible that he bought later: *'J Symons. Sgt. May 12, 1934'*; and, in a finer, educated hand, in a combined *Book of Common Prayer* and *Hymns Ancient and Modern: 'J Symons. Saugor, CP. January 20th 1940.'*

It is there, in the Prayer Book, in the underlining that he made in his favourite psalms and hymns. There is an especially emphatic marking beside hymn 176:

> *'How sweet the name of* JESUS *sounds*
> *In a believer's ear!*
> *It soothes his sorrows, heals his wounds*
> *And drives away his fears.'*

Above the hymn is printed a quotation from the New Testament: *'unto you therefore which believe He is precious'*.

Was it all in vain?

What I saw and heard and felt in those times was as bad as anything I have ever known. A distinguished consultant neurologist in London later told me that he regarded it as the worst illness that he knew. Of course, it affected my own hopes for a healthy life and more besides, but at that time such thoughts about myself did not come to me. It was what I saw in Dad alone that found every target in me.

And there is one parallel that I know of which helps me understand this. It is when, at the end of all things – or so it seemed – Jesus, tortured and nailed to the Cross, calls to his Father: *'My God, My God, why hast Thou forsaken me?'*

He utters a loud cry: *'It is all completed,'* and He dies; He is finished.

When Jesus uttered His cry of dereliction, of abandonment, was He asking, 'What have I done, God, to cause you to abandon me?' Or was he asking, 'To what purpose have You abandoned me?'

No, it was not the first. For Jesus did not believe that His Heavenly Father rewarded sin with disaster, or goodness with success. His Father makes the sun to shine and the rain to fall equally on the just and the unjust. When a crowd surrounding Jesus were complaining about His interest in a crippled man who had probably, they said, brought his misfortune on himself, Jesus healed him. The purpose of the affliction was that He might show God's mercy and healing. So, in his cry of dereliction, Jesus was perhaps asking about the purpose of God in his Passion.

For his part, Dad did not ask, in my hearing, 'Why me?' There is no answer to that. Huntington's just happens, like so many other things to so many people.

But that Dad's suffering had a meaning and purpose, I am clear. Its meaning was the way he and Mum behaved; in their goodness they revealed God's goodness. They kept their eyes on that and somehow found a meaning in it all. With that faith, and for the sake of their children, they could endure all things.

In my heart I know only one way to understand what happened to Dad. I remember all that he had done and achieved against terrible odds; the integrity with which he had done it; the way he saw through to the bitter end what he undertook – loving us to the uttermost, even when, at moments, I regarded him as living yet dead.

For this is what Dad means to me, the manner in which he continued to live for us for twenty years after the worst began to happen:

'Take to heart what you found in Christ Jesus.
He was in the form of God,
yet He reckoned that no reason for grasping for Himself,
but made Himself nothing,
taking the form of a slave.
Bearing human likeness, sharing the human lot,
He humbled himself, and was obedient, even to death,
death on a cross.
Therefore God raised Him to the heights
and bestowed on Him the name above all names ...
to the glory of God the Father.'

St Paul, Epistle to the Philippians, Ch 2, v 5-11

Dad did, indeed, take that message to heart. What Dad did, how he lived as one of Jesus' followers, mirrored Jesus' way. And Dad's death, like that of the One Whom he followed, was not the end.

Epilogue

THIRTY YEARS LATER, on 1st August 2002, Ralf and Peggy, Judy and I are setting off on a special walk. We are on holiday at Ringmore, a village about a mile from the sea at Challaborough.

With haversacks, cameras, binoculars and map, we walk past All Hallows church, with its square, grey tower and a small black spire perched on top of it, and then make our way along the narrow lanes to the small village of Kingston. We buy stamps in the Methodist church, which functions as a post office on two mornings a week, and then have lunch in the garden at the Dolphin Inn.

Meeting not a soul, we take the National Trust footpath and then join the coastal path at Fernycombe Point. From there we can see the waters of the estuary of the River Erme (so treacherous to swimmers) and the yellow, empty sands of the private beach at Mothecombe.

We climb the cliff path to Hoist Point, over three hundred feet above the sea, and we see the tors of Dartmoor, twenty miles to the north. To the south, twenty-six miles out at sea, is the Eddystone lighthouse, standing out sharply and clearly, well within the horizon granted us by the height of the cliffs and the clear air.

We are enjoying the secret, perfect weather of south Devon, the freshness and sunshine afforded by a low-pressure system, while the rest of the country suffers floods. It was often like this at the caravan at Challaborough in the 1950s and 1960s.

The smell of the sea, the warmth of the air and the fragrance of the grass on the cliffs cast a spell on us. The close-cropped turf puts a spring in our step and lifts our hearts.

As we walk, with the fields on our left hand and the sea on our right, Ralf points out the buzzards high above us, mewing as they teach their young how to hunt; swallows and swifts, screaming in flight as they catch insects. The swifts are staying on rather later than usual this year. In a few spots we see cirl buntings, unique to this coast.

In the hedges there are banks of wild flowers: great mullein, purple toadflax, pink-purple toadflax, yellow toadflax, mugwort, hedge woundwort, enchanter's nightshade, pink perslane, hedge bedstraw, tufted vetch, fleabane, pineapple mayweed, fumitory, corn marigold; as well as the more common flowers, herb Robert, red campion, honeysuckle, scarlet pimpernel, speedwell, hawkbit and common cleavers.

At one stage, near the copse at Broad Cliff where Freshwater Brook plunges about a hundred feet straight down to the beach, a new path turns a little inland and tacks back and forth, in order to make the sheer slopes easier for walkers.

Ralf recalls how, forty years ago, almost to the day, he walked this coast when the path still kept close to the cliff edge. On this section there had been steps, cut into the hillside.

Dad was with Ralf on that strenuous climb.

The two of them did the whole of the walk together, making a long hike from Challaborough via Ringmore, Kingston, Blackaport Cross, the path on the eastern bank of the Erme and then the cliffs, and back to the caravan. It amounts to fifteen miles in all, walked with only a drink of water from a tap in a farmyard. It is Ralf's most precious memory of Dad.

Today the weather is perfect but we meet no one on the cliff path. Yet I sense another person in step with us on this walk.

Appendix

Huntington's Chorea

A RELATIVELY RARE, hereditary neurological disease that is characterised by irregular and involuntary movements of the muscles. It is caused by a genetic mutation that causes degeneration of neurons in a part of the brain that controls movement ... Symptoms of mental deterioration begin later ... There is no effective therapy or cure, and the disease invariably proves fatal. A child of a person with Huntington's chorea has a fifty per cent chance of developing the disease.

Britannica Concise Encyclopedia, 2002

Huntington's disease lasts around twenty years.

Oliver Quarrell, Huntington's Disease: The Facts, Oxford University Press, 1999

The body gradually becomes engulfed in a panoply of abnormal movements. Mood alters, usually becoming depressed to the point of suicide, occasionally becoming manic, often irritable, explosive, hypersensitive, withdrawn and apathetic ... Thinking, reasoning, organising become disrupted; judgement goes awry; memory is impaired, but some insight into their own and their family's conditions, and even a sense of humour, can be maintained until the end. Speech is lost, independent care is impossible, and death a welcome relief.

N. Wexler, in *Psychological Aspects of Genetic Counselling*, edited by A.E.H. Emery and I.M. Pullens, London: Academic Press, 1984

Family Tree

representing those members of the family who are most frequently mentioned

MY GREAT-GRANDPARENTS

John Hocking SYMONS*	=	Peace CRAWSHAW	Susan SAUNDRY / GROVES	Elijah JARROLD	=	Emma IDEN	Charles ALDERSEY	=	Elizabeth WARD
d.1907		d.1931	d.1900	d.1892		d.1874	d.?		d.1909
aged 66		aged 80	aged 48	aged 50		aged 28	aged ?		aged 76

MY GRANDPARENTS

William*	=	Florence Louisa	Henry	=	Agnes
d.1914		d.1921	d.1939		d.1943
aged 36		aged 39	aged 72		aged 76

Three brothers:
Frank*
Ernest m. Ellen
Alfred m. Maud

Six sisters:
Florrie, Suzie
Nora, Rene,
Clara,* Kathleen*

DAD*
(known as Jack in the family,
and as Bill in the Army)
d.1972
aged 70

MUM
(Grace)
d.1998
aged 88

Five brothers:
Harry, George,
Jack, Arthur, Walter
Two sisters: Edith, Hilda

MY COUSINS

Auntie Florrie married Charlie, who introduced Dad and Mum. Their children were Terry, Jack, Doris and Coulson. Auntie Clara and her husband, also called Charlie, had five children, of whom only Barbara has not contracted Huntington's disease.

Auntie Hilda married Fred. Their son is my cousin John. Auntie Edith (Edie) married Len. Their daughter was my cousin Mavis; their son is my cousin Gerald.

* Suffered from Huntington's disease. (William carried the gene, but died before symptoms appeared.)

Acknowledgements

LINES FROM *The White Cliffs of Dover*, by Alice Duer Miller, published by Methuen, 1941, are reproduced by permission of Pollinger Limited and the Estate of Alice Duer Miller.

An excerpt from *A Shaft of Sunlight* by Philip Mason, published by Andre Deutsch, 1979, is reproduced by permission of Mr Mason's family.

An excerpt from *George* by Emlyn Williams, published by Hamish Hamilton, 1961, is reproduced by permission of Mr Williams' literary executors, c/o the Maggie Nash Literary Agency.

An excerpt from the *Britannica Concise Encyclopaedia*, 2002, is reproduced by permission of the publisher.

An excerpt from *Huntington's Disease: The Facts*, by Oliver Quarrell, 1999, is reproduced by permission of Oxford University Press.

An excerpt from an article by Nancy S. Wexler in *Psychological Aspects of Genetic Counselling*, edited by A.E.H. Emery and I.M. Pullens, London: Academic Press, 1984, is reproduced by permission of Dr Wexler.